America's New
Women Entrepreneurs

America's New
Women
Entrepreneurs

Tips, Tactics, and Techniques of Women Achievers in Business

Foreword by Linda Evans

Edited by Patricia Harrison

Introduction by Cathleen Black

ACROPOLIS BOOKS LTD.
WASHINGTON, D.C.

ACROPOLIS BOOKS, LTD.
Colortone Building, 2400 17th St., N.W.,
Washington, D.C. 20009

Printed in the United States of America by
COLORTONE PRESS
Creative Graphics, Inc.
Washington, D.C. 20009

Attention: Schools and Corporations
ACROPOLIS books are available at
quantity discounts with bulk purchase for
educational, business, or sales promotional use. For information, please write
to: SPECIAL SALES DEPARTMENT,
ACROPOLIS BOOKS, LTD.,2400 17th
ST., N.W., WASHINGTON, D.C. 20009

**Are there Acropolis Books you want but
cannot find in your local stores?**
You can get any Acropolis book title in
print. Simply send title and retail price,
plus $1.50 cents per copy to cover mailing
and handling costs for each book desired.
District of Columbia residents add
applicable sales tax. Enclose check or
money order only, no cash please, to:
ACROPOLIS BOOKS LTD., 2400 17th
ST., N.W., WASHINGTON, D.C. 20009.

Library of Congress Cataloging-in-Publication Data

Harrison, Patricia, 1943-
    America's new women entrepreneurs.

    Includes index.
    1. Success in business.   2. Women in business.
I. Title.
HF5386.H287   1986   658.4'2   86-8037
ISBN 0-87491-810-3

Contents

Contents

Foreword

As someone who has worked all of her life, I can identify not only with the women in this book, but also with the women who will be inspired by these stories. The women you are about to meet can become, for you, as they have for me, a source of renewal and inspiration. Today they are all successful businesswomen but it was not always so. In many cases their success was built on tragedy and disappointment. Marilyn Hamilton was paralyzed in a hang-gliding accident, Ellen Terry was deserted by her husband and unable to support her children, Lynette Spano Vives began dreaming as a small child in Brooklyn of ways to escape the pattern of poverty encompassing her family.

All of them broke through their roadblocks, met the challenge, and took charge of their own lives. How they did it can inspire and provide women with the encouragement and courage to begin now.

These new female entrepreneurs allow us to look behind the curtain of their success and understand how they came through the struggle in a winning way for themselves and their families. Their advice has been hard won, based on real life experiences, and will give you a ruler with which to gauge your own entrepreneurial abilities.

The important thing to remember is that, yes, you can do it too. It doesn't matter what your age, race, education, or social status is—if you have the desire to begin, and the commitment to follow through, you will join the new growing list of successful women entrepreneurs.

Linda Evans
Actress and Businesswoman

Preface

 W e have come a long way. The collective achievements represented in *America's New Female Entrepreneurs*—both the personal journeys and the professional arrivals— are a cause for celebration.

The women included in this book are part of the wave of women who changed a critical aspect of American business— not how American business works, but who is working in it. We created new opportunities and provided the resources to fill them as women in business. We have moved from the delegated to the delegators, from the followers to the leaders.

This progression from followers in business to leaders, in less than a generation, could only have happened within the American free enterprise system. When we began to assert our talent and confidence, we found that many doors were closed to us. They were closed but not locked. Some of us pried open the doors and joined the ranks of previously all male corporate suites. Other women bypassed the doors, climbed through the windows, and founded their own businesses. The point is, the American system gave us places to start. It may have been a different place, in some cases it paid less than for our male colleagues, but opportunity was there for us.

Today it is not so much the issue of men and women as it is the changing of the free enterprise guard, regardless of which gender is at the helm. American corporate leadership is moving from standardization to innovation, from autocracy to consensus, from the corporate protectionism of management ideas to the free trade of ideas. Business and industry and government are more competitive than ever before. This is why women are becoming more visible in corporate power positions and as entrepreneurs. We are making it to the top because successful business demands the best talent it can get. *It's that simple.* Business and industry and government cannot afford to ignore the talent of more than half of the population.

Fifteen years ago, American business was forced to acknowledge our presence. Ten years ago, it began to accept our middle management skill support. Today, it deserves our leadership in companies and boards, as entrepreneurs, as top management. The free enterprise system needs our contribution and we have responded with talent, energy and dedication.

I am encouraged by these stories and I encourage all of you to acknowledge your own talents and move forward with your dream whether it is to own your own business or become chief executive officer of a Fortune 500 company. The opportunity is as wide as your vision.

Cathleen Black
Publisher, *USA Today*

Introduction

The National Women's Economic Alliance, an organization comprising men and women leaders from business, industry, and government who work together to identify ways to increase women's career and economic opportunities within the free enterprise system, is very pleased to introduce you to *America's New Women Entrepreneurs.*

The women you are about to meet affirm the significant contribution that American women have made and are continuing to make to the success of the free enterprise system. According to Webster's Dictionary, the true definition of entrepreneur is "one who organizes and takes responsibility for a business enterprise in order to make a profit." Within this book you will meet many "enterprising women," although not all of them run their own companies. Whether you are enterprising on your own or working for a corporation, you will find that the skills women business owners demonstrate in running a business are equally important to women who are targeting a career within the corporation.

I believe this book will encourage you to identify your own special strengths and talents, have confidence that you too have a contribution to make, and show you some of the ways you might move forward with your dream and overcome the roadblocks of procrastination, fear, and doubt that prevent success. As Mary Crowley, president and chief executive officer, Home Interiors and Gifts, Inc., says, "What does a roadblock tell you? That the road continues on the other side."

What *America's New Women Entrepreneurs* demonstrates is that women are naturals when it comes to business. Whether you find their entrepreneurial talents within industry or as heads of their own companies, one thing is clear—all those years of organizing and being responsible for others have finally paid off. We know how to run things and we are running successfully.

To get the most out of this book I think it is important to identify what key elements are important in order to achieve in business. You will find what they are by turning to the "Tips for Success" at the end of each profile. One essential ingredient is commitment. It is clear that success cannot be achieved on a nine-to-five basis.

Another key ingredient for the successful entrepreneur is self-confidence. As you learn about these successful women you'll realize that in many cases they acted a lot more confidently than they actually felt—and true confidence followed.

Whether you are starting out in the workforce or you are a long-time worker, I believe you will be inspired and encouraged by this book. The women you are about to meet have very little in common, except one thing—they all wanted something better and they all wanted to be the best that they could be. This quest to achieve their potential kept them going around, under, and through roadblocks of prejudice, physical handicap, lack of money, no education, and little encouragement to a fulfillment no amount of money can buy—self-actualization. Contrary to the old cliché, getting richer did not make them unhappy people. Their personal success enabled them to be more effective in helping others succeed.

Marge Schott was able to say thank you to the people of Cincinnati by buying the Cincinnati Reds and keeping the team in Cincinnati; Marilyn Hamilton's ultralight wheelchairs have enabled thousands of disabled men, women, and children to have increased mobility; Mary Crowley continues to contribute to her community through Home Interiors scholarships, education, and youth programs; Ellen Terry works with teenagers who have drug abuse problems; and the list goes on.

I hope *America's New Women Entrepreneurs* will encourage you to identify and claim your opportunity for success. Don't be afraid of failure; don't be afraid to take risks. And, most important, don't be afraid to begin!

Patricia Harrison

President, The National Women's Economic Alliance

Acknowledgments

Special thanks to Daniel V. Cusimano, appreciation to Emily McKhann and Felicia Rappoport, E. Bruce Harrison Company, for interviews in Washington and across the country.

Our appreciation to those corporations who made the research for this book possible: The Alcoa Foundation; Allied-Signal Corporation; Amoco Foundation; Clairol, Inc.; Conoco; Dow Chemical Company; Exxon Company, USA; Edison Electric Institute; The Hanes Group; Chevron USA; Nestle Enterprises, Inc.; Rockwell International; Sara Lee Corporation; Sears Roebuck and Company; and U.S. Steel Corporation.

The Alliance Committee comprising Geraldine Cox, Chemical Manufacturers Association; Renee Ross, Center For Office Technology; Maria Siravo, General Electric Company; Melinda Farris, Capital Connections; Zoe Coulson, The Campbell Soup Company; Mary Noel Walker, Sheraton Washington, ITT Corporation, established the following criteria for the women profiled:

1. A record of significant personal and professional achievement in her career.

2. A record of significant contribution to business, corporate, or free enterprise standards and accomplishment.

3. A record of sharing her experience and counsel with others interested in or pursuing careers within the free enterprise system.

4. Achievement of measurable goals and demonstrated leadership ability within the free enterprise system.

5. Demonstration of continuing commitment to free enterprise wherever employed.

P.S.H.

> **"Lupe Anguiano has had to battle government intervention to help welfare mothers take pride in themselves and become self-sufficient."**

Lupe Anguiano
Founder, President,
National Women's Employment
and Education, Inc.
San Antonio, Texas

For fifteen years, I was a Catholic nun. I entered the religious life when I was twenty and left at thirty-five. I married a few years later but the marriage lasted only one year. My focus now is twofold—union with God and the ability to help women currently on welfare find new dignity and success in their lives.

Raised on the Work Ethic

I was born in Lajunta, Colorado. My father worked on the railroad, and every year we would go to California where my aunt lived to pick crops for the summer. Then we would go back to Colorado after the walnut season ended in September. The important thing for me is that I don't ever remember *not* working. Working was always a part of our family. It was a contribution we could all make and I was proud of it.

Education was very valued by my family especially since my sister and I were the first in the family to graduate from high school. My older sister and brother had to leave school early and get jobs that would help our family survive. I'll never forget the tears in my father's eyes when we walked down the aisle at our graduation.

My mother had the greatest influence in my life. She succeeded because she lived what she taught me, both spiritually and in business. She taught me that love, happiness, and success are within everyone's reach—if you really want to attain them. In business, she was able to restart a small store in Saticoy, California, with money she saved from our migrant work. If you know what a migrant worker makes, you know how much she had to sacrifice to save for that store. She had lost her business during the Mexican revolution when she had to flee to the United States.

My mother and father came to this country after the Mexican revolution with nothing except the clothes on their backs. Yet they had that determination to succeed. My father worked on the railroad, my mother ran her store, and we all helped.

Family Pride

The element that helped me the most in using my talents was a family pride—a family push. Working was a great part of that pride or strength. Because I knew firsthand how important it was for each individual to believe in his or her abilities, to have pride, to have courage, I knew how enervating it could be to the human spirit to have to depend upon public welfare or assistance.

Through my work on a government committee I was able to find out just how demoralizing it is for women to depend on welfare and public assistance. It is the complete opposite of the self-esteem that comes from being an entrepreneur.

The message I heard from women on public assistance was that welfare was dehumanizing. I heard them express a desire to work, to become self-supporting. They wanted to help themselves become self-supporting. They told me that they needed information about available jobs. They wanted skills training, temporary help with child care, and transportation. They needed these support services as they became established within the workforce.

I started to lobby for these changes. My argument was that Aid to Families with Dependent Children (AFDC) needed to focus on employment training coupled with minor temporary emergency assistance to help stabilize female single parents in jobs, rather than give them income support with additional social services and then refuse to allow them to work. Obviously these suggestions and ideas were not accepted in Congress in 1972, and, as a matter of fact, some Congressional members treated these recommendations as totally out of line.

National Women's Employment and Education, Inc.

I resigned my position in Washington in 1973 and moved to San Antonio, Texas, accepting a position as southwest regional director with the Catholic bishops. I made AFDC reform my priority issue. I moved into the San Antonio Public Housing Projects and started to assist women on AFDC move into the workforce.

I founded National Women's Employment and Education, Inc., a nonprofit organization, and developed a model program with the assistance of private employers. My corporation is funded with grants from Con Edison, American Express, J.C. Penney, Chase Manhattan Bank, and others. The program is based on job training. Entry level jobs are found in the private sector and women are matched with these jobs. Child care and transporation are arranged so the women can concentrate on their jobs. Our program also guides each woman through employment readiness classes and employment interviews. Once the woman has been placed in a job we stand by available to help with problems and conflicts. My reward is seeing welfare dependent women become proud and self-supporting individuals.

I have tested this program in both the public and private sectors. In San Antonio, where it has been implemented with private funds, it has worked very well, but in Dallas and Ventura, California, where I allowed it to be implemented with public funds, it did not work.

The greatest obstacle is competing with existing government-supported social delivery systems. It is very difficult to retain an innovative, superior private sector employment method. I find government always wants to control or convince you that their method is very similar to yours—and therefore you should join them. I have turned down government funds because they wanted to change effective programs.

Insufficient Social Delivery Systems

I feel strongly that our country's social delivery systems patronize the poor. In general, I think the majority of social service delivery systems destroy human dignity. Most are based on charity giving, rather than assisting the poor to become self-sufficient.

Our country has so many nonprofit organizations making a living off poor people's misery, that the best I can offer existing social service delivery systems is an example—an effective model that they can use within the system.

My goal for the next five years is to change AFDC welfare from public assistance to economic self-sufficiency through employment. The women's employment and education model program is, in my opinion, the future of AFDC welfare.

Better Employment Methods

This is in the process of being accomplished by developing national demonstration models in New York and Los Angeles, strictly with private support. When they are done, I will challenge all communities to do what we have done with private support. I will do this from my home in San Antonio. It is crucial that we discover better employment methods for serving the unemployed or the so-called hard-core unemployed. We can learn from both private sector employers and women employees how best to work together so that benefits accrue to everyone participating in the program. It has taken me ten years to create this model program and I hope one day to see it used as a national employment formula for women and single heads of households who are currently being supported by AFDC welfare.

The best marketing tool, whether you are in the private or nonprofit sector, is delivering an excellent product. I believe my corporation has an excellent product and we will succeed. Persistence and focus plus hard work have always been key qualities in any success I have enjoyed. I have not allowed major setbacks to discourage my efforts to succeed. In fact, I view all obstacles as learning steps toward the goal. The goal: to create a national effective, economical, and humane employment system for 85 percent of our nation's women single parents on AFDC welfare.

When the Women's Employment and Education Model Program moves these 85 percent into jobs, I plan to go into the manufacturing and designing of southwestern clothes and organize this business as an innovative profit-sharing corporation.

Young women ask me how to succeed. I answer that hard work and determination are the answer; with focus and determination you can succeed. Living in a private enterprise system opens the door to using your energies. There is nothing holding you back. In a private enterprise system you are encouraged to get ahead—it is great. I think everyone was created to succeed in life.

TIPS FOR SUCCESS

1. Focus on what you want to accomplish and you can do it. That is the only way that you can actually do something, and do it well—if you have goals.
2. Looking at millionaires in this country, I see that very few had college degrees. They all started through hard work and determination. That supercedes all else, and should be your strong point.

"A belief that a business based on the golden rule could succeed inspired Mary Kay Ash.**"**

Mary Kay Ash
Chairman, Mary Kay Cosmetics
Dallas, Texas

After I retired from a career in direct sales in 1963, I decided to write my memoirs, a book that would help other women overcome some of the obstacles I had encountered. First, I wrote down all of the good things the companies I had been with had done and then the changes I would make. I began to dream of a company that would give women the opportunity to do everything they were smart enough to do, a company that cared about working mothers, cared about their customers. A company based on the golden rule. Today, we call it the "go-give" principle. We focus on giving, not getting.

A Dream Company

I kept thinking what it would be like if someone would actually start such a company. That was really the beginning of Mary Kay Cosmetics. The product line would be skin care—the very products I had used faithfully for twenty-five years.

In the early fifties, I was a demonstrator for Stanley Home Products. The twenty women attending the Stanley party ranged in ages from early twenties to seventies. As I demonstrated the Stanley Products, I kept looking at the women gathered there and wondered how it was possible for twenty women of such varied ages to all have peaches and cream complexions. Their skin was really fantastic.

After the party was over, I watched as the hostess gave these women individual jars with black tops and penciled labels. When I asked her about the jars she told me that the women were using a special cream and she was following their skin progress. The cream was based on a formula owned by the woman's father. He was a hide tanner who became very curious about the fact that his hands looked younger than his face. He discovered that the hide-tanning solution he was using was working on his hands in a positive way. After all, if the solution could turn big-pored, stiff hides into beautiful, small-pored soft glove leather, then perhaps the formula could work wonders with skin as well. He began to experiment with the formula, adapting its strength for skin application. Did it work? When he died at seventy-five he had the skin of a much younger man.

My experience with this formula was successful too and I bought the secret from his daughter. Now, my dream company was on its way.

Opportunities for Women

I had a product and I had the drive and energy to make my business successful but I wanted one more thing. I wanted to help women achieve. My frustrations as a woman in the business world were based on the fact that I had often been paid far less than a man doing the same work. Many times I had trained a salesman and after months of guiding and teaching him on the road, he was brought back to Dallas and made my superior at twice my salary! The reason I was given was that these men had families to support. No one seemed to care that I had a family to support also.

I wanted a company that would respect the contribution women could make. I knew we were smart and capable, honest and committed. Couldn't my new company recognize these talents? My company would offer women opportunities that in 1963 didn't exist anywhere else. I knew there was a vast, unlimited amount of talent and dedication to hard work that had never been tapped before—simply because these talented and dedicated people were women.

A Cash Basis System

My dream company would let women set their own ceiling on how much they could earn. At Mary Kay, we have worked out a system where our consultants and directors pay in advance for their merchandise with a cashier's check or money order. The director never runs up a debt with the company. This means we have few accounts receivable and don't have the expense of collecting bad debts. This system benefits our sales people because we pass the savings on to them in the form of higher commissions. Our salespeople, in addition to improving their self-image, can earn in three hours what they would normally earn in eight, no matter what their profession.

Our entire business philosophy is based on the golden rule. We treat people as we would like to be treated—and everyone benefits. Each person is important.

I believe that we have gathered together a group of people who believe in our company, believe in our product, and believe in themselves—and they in turn go out and find others who share our belief. Ours is a shared success and that's the best kind. My definition of happiness is, first, having work that you love to do, something you love so much you'd do it even if you weren't paid; second, having someone to love; and, third, having something to look forward to. I like what Ralph Waldo Emerson said: "Nothing great was ever achieved without enthusiasm." At Mary Kay we know it's true.

TIPS FOR SUCCESS

1. Never pass up an opportunity to better yourself.
2. If you have a dream, pursue it. Don't let the rest of the world tell you what to do about it.
3. Keep saying to yourself, "I can do it." If you say it long enough, you *will* do it.
4. Put your best effort into everything you do.
5. Compete with yourself. Strive to get that extra special effort out of yourself.
6. Get someone else to do the things that aren't important for you to do personally. This means, whenever possible, to delegate your work. Stop spending dollar time on penny jobs.
7. Set realistic short-term goals you can attain and go on to bigger ones as you gain confidence in your ability.
8. Fail forward to success. It is impossible to avoid mistakes. Learn from them and never give up. Remember, obstacles either polish us up or wear us down.
9. The best reason to start a new company is that there is a need for what you have to offer. Ask yourself what you really do well and start thinking about doing it in terms of a business.
10. The only difference between successful people and unsuccessful people is extraordinary determination.

"From the Depression, Norma Beasley moved upward, with a dream, determination, and a golden rule.**"**

Norma Lea Beasley
Chairman,
Chief Executive Officer,
SAFECO Land Title of Dallas
Dallas, Texas

I believe I started off with the ingredients for an American success story as the firstborn to struggling new parents against the backdrop of rural America. The time: the Depression. Some people would regard this as a scenario for failure but I always knew I was going to succeed. Who I am and what I have achieved can be attributed directly to character traits developed in early childhood, under the guidance of my parents.

Early Lessons

My father had just purchased a tract of land with the help of a hefty bank loan when the Depression struck. He and my mother were living in a converted one-car garage when I was born. When my sister was born two and a half years later, father added what he could afford—another room—making it a two-room home.

Father was embarrassed because he could not give us a big two-story house like the one he lived in as a child. He was always saying, "One of these days I will buy you all the finest home in the country." He finally did just before my tenth birthday when he bought the land and the big house on it next to where we were living . That home, and our expanded holdings, were proof to me that a dream could become a reality. This was probably the most important lesson I ever learned.

We were fruit growers. Father shipped our apples to market and came home with saddles, clocks, guns, and very little money. When Highway 71 opened in front of our house, he realized we could retail our own fruit for more profit. The packing shed became an ever-expanding roadside stand and we all worked in it. I could sell and give correct change before I'd started school.

Father's ingenuity was matched by his honesty and sense of fair play. He stressed that the apples at the bottom of the basket had to be as good as those at top, and we must always give full measure. As his credo, "Do unto others as you would have them do unto you," became known, our business grew. We began selling our friends and neighbors fruits and vegetables, and by helping others helped ourselves even more. I quickly learned the rewards of abiding by the golden rule.

We worked long hours, seven days a week. We gave out late at night, but we never gave up. My sister and I were taught that if a job was worth doing, it was worth giving your all. Consequently, I would boss workers who weren't working constantly during our harvest. This sometimes resulted in my being paddled by my father. I soon learned to assume authority only when it was rightfully mine.

Father involved us in everything, even decisions. He sought and respected mother's business opinions. Soon he received my views as well. Sometimes my opinions were well-received, sometimes not; but they were always heard. His explanations taught me reasoning.

At six, I started school and was quickly promoted because I'd already learned so much. My grade school years were pretty uneventful. My dreams of what I wanted to do when I grew up changed weekly when I went to the Saturday night movies in town.

Responsibility came by age nine when my father was buying and paying for carloads of apples based on my count of the bushels as they were unloaded. I was never really treated as a child. If I thought a job might be too tough, I felt challenged to find a way to do it. I did not always succeed; I learned the limitations of my ability, too.

Deciding on a Career

My first day of high school was a momentous one. That morning had been so dreadful: rain water was still running off the cow that came into my milking stall. Flies were swarming and she was swatting them, and me, with her wet tail full of cockleburs. Then she kicked at them and hit the milk bucket, splashing milk all over me and knocking me back into the mess she'd just made. That did it. I had had my fill of farm life. Later in school when the civics teacher opened his class by asking us what we wanted to be I glanced at the book's first chapter, "Lawyers as Good Law Makers," and I replied: "A lawyer."

Once my public proclamation was made, there was no turning back. Father, who'd been chairman of the local school board for years, had hoped I would be a teacher. My decision to be a lawyer was not considered a wise one. Even my favorite teacher, who always had my best interests in mind, tried to convince me that it would be too difficult. Her husband, who was in engineering at the University of Arkansas, related how hard his buddies in law school were struggling.

Undaunted, I enrolled in the University of Arkansas when I was still sixteen years old. Because of a still unrequited interest in art, I chose the College of Arts and Sciences. My high school grades were not outstanding, but I had made the honor roll and upper 10 percent of the class easily. Now, for the first time, I learned the meaning of study and preparation. I struggled, but survived. At age eighteen, I entered the School of Law where our class of seventy-four was told that only one in five would graduate. When many glanced meaningfully at me, I only became more determined.

That determination was put to a severe test my second semester when my father suffered a paralyzing stroke and I took over management of the farm and produce business. Thankfully, many of my fellow students became big brothers and supported me, even against teachers who gave me a bad time. True to the prediction, we graduated a class of seventeen. I became a licensed attorney before the end of my twenty-first year.

First Job

My toughest "real life" learning experience was my first job, with a large Oklahoma oil company. I was not only the first female attorney, but the youngest ever hired. The little country girl away from home for the first time, restricted to an office high off the ground, felt like a caged animal. My secretary was twenty-seven, thought she knew more than I, and actually did, to my chagrin. That produced another first; I questioned myself. Why had I worked myself away from friends, family, and a life I knew and loved? I left this unsuccessful experience telling myself it was necessary to attend Suburban Methodist University Graduate School of Law to learn more about my chosen field: oil and gas law.

I expected Dallas to welcome me with open arms, offering a great job in the oil and gas industry. Wrong again. Dallas oil companies required their attorneys to apprentice in the leasing field, and all considered this work too dangerous for a woman. I would not go home in defeat. I was determined to stay in Dallas and did so by working at temporary bookkeeping jobs.

Stumbling onto a New Interest

Finally in desperation, I accepted a job in an industry in which I had no interest: title insurance. The company manager promised to teach me the business if I would do whatever needed doing. One of my first duties was relieving the receptionist. This steady job enabled me to enroll in the SMU graduate courses I wanted at night.

Admission rules had just changed however, and I was required to complete an undergraduate degree. Still knowing no boundaries, I petitioned the University of Arkansas to allow me to complete one year of undergraduate studies in real estate and business at SMU and transfer the credits back to complete my B.S. in Law. I obtained that degree and took and passed the Texas bar exam the same year. By the time I completed the coursework for a master's in oil and gas, I had lost interest in the field because I had progressed so far in the title business.

My employer fired the head of the legal department and gave me the title for a job I'd already done for two years. But I still earned only half what the man had for the same job. When the head of the company told me that the only way a woman would get ahead in business would be to have a "lap job" on the side, I walked. Again, I had been challenged.

I joined a company owned by two of the most respected men in the title industry, as the head of their legal department. My rise to vice-president, general counsel, and, finally, executive vice-president, at the age of thirty-five, was really enjoyable. I was so proud of the titles—I don't believe any other woman was executive vice-president of a major Dallas title company without ownership interest. But I was ignoring the question of salary, never letting that unfortunate aspect of the job affect the quality of my work.

When one of the partners sold his interest to a major title insurance company, the new owners promoted the remaining partner to president but questioned the wisdom of having a woman as executive vice-president. They asked me and a male employee to submit to testing by their management experts. I never learned my scores, but was confirmed as executive vice-president and general counsel. Nearly a year later, another employee advised me that they had been shocked by my high scores.

Growing Ambition

In the meantime, my ambition and dreams grew unchecked. I was earning extra money by teaching business law and real estate courses at SMU's downtown campus. I decided I knew enough about the title business to start my own company, and even dreamed of owning a string of such companies across Texas. I infected two friends, an abstractor and an accountant, with my enthusiasm for this dream. We formed a free-lance abstract service company in an adjacent county and prepared to open a title company plant. In 1965, that company opened, with my friend, Imogene Walker, a CPA, as president and me as chairman of the board and CEO—my first top titles—self-promoted.

During this time I was also teaching courses for the Board of Realtors, advising realtors, and expanding my contact network. When the real estate license law was revised to include education requirements, I was hired in 1967 by the Dallas County Community Colleges to establish real estate schools on two campuses, under the auspices of the community service program.

When a business associate bought a title company in 1967, planning to become its chairman and CEO but leaving top management intact, he asked me to join his management team. I could see the brick wall looming up there and declined. I didn't want any more battle bruises.

Striking Out Alone

A year later, he approached me again, suggesting I open an attorney closing office with which he would do business. The prospect was appealing, but doing it was scary. I forfeited my nice titles and secure salary. It was one thing to start a new business as an investment while holding down a steady job, but quite another to strike out alone with no guaranteed source of income.

My worries were unfounded. In the past few years, I had made many contacts who now became clients. And my time was now my own. I continued teaching in the evenings and invested my surplus funds in rental real estate. Free of the previous conflict of interest possibilities, I concentrated on expanding the title company chain. My partners and I opened companies number two and three in two surrounding counties.

My closing business grew steadily and I eventually purchased the building in which I'd started in a small office. This was in 1973, the beginning of a three-year real estate recession. But risks didn't faze me. I even purchased my dream home then. My love affair with real estate and fellow attorneys was paying off. As usual, success was a direct result of my work ethic. Clients appreciated the fact that I would work seven days a week, if necessary, to serve them properly.

During this period I did learn some prudence. My dream of owning a state-wide chain was fading as I tried unsuccessfully to manage an Austin title firm I'd purchased. I realized it was smarter to keep my business interests closer to home and more manageable. So, our partnership purchased a fourth title plant in an adjacent county.

In 1975, Paul Pulliam, an attorney who had represented one of my best customers prior to the recession, asked me for a job. (He'd always kidded me about needing some male influence in my all female office.) After some thought, I offered to make him a partner in a title closing operation. This new firm quickly grew beyond all expectations.

A potential partner approached us in 1977 and we soon joined him in ownership of a fifth title company. We took in another partner and opened a sixth company a year later.

Lucky Number Seven

By now, we had our home county, Dallas, surrounded. Opening a firm here would be the biggest risk I'd ever taken, so I was studying a number of possibilities. Then Pulliam and I were approached by the California-based SAFECO Title Insurance Company to provide attorney closing services for their relatively new operation in Dallas. That gave me a much better idea: number seven, my lucky number seven. I discussed my idea with my banker who agreed to supply, somehow, the estimated $1.5 million I might need.

On the flight to California, I popped the question to Pulliam. I asked him if he would join CPA Walker and me in what I considered to be the perfect team to buy and manage a successful title company in Dallas, the SAFECO operation. His first reaction was to laugh; then he proceeded to tell me there was no chance they'd want to sell a plant they'd just gone to great lengths to acquire. There it was: another challenge. I was ready to charge ahead. My qualms about the purchase vanished, despite the urging by Pulliam and another associate that we really should be *joining* SAFECO.

The following day we met with the corporate officers of SAFECO to hear their proposal. I immediately advised them that I would not be interested in moving my office as there were not sufficient advantages to offset potential difficulties; it was just a lateral move for me. Then, I offered them a proposal: they should sell their Dallas company to us.

After pointing out how poor their business had been in the first year and how another, older title insurance firm was still not profitable, I explained how the 6 percent of the business they had and what I could bring in would turn their loss into a half-million dollar gain in the first year. I emphasized how our reputation and success could help them build a network of good independent agents in Texas, where they were so eager to expand. Plus, I promised them business from the six independent agencies I owned.

Golden Rule Result

This all fell on deaf ears. They made counter-proposals that I politely rejected, reiterating the logic of selling to us. After a recess, we reconvened for lunch with their president, Bill Little. He sat down next to me and immediately said, "I hear you've come out here to buy our Dallas company." As we ate, I repeated my offer and supporting arguments, with two purchase options. He cleared his throat to get the large table's attention and said, "Miss Beasley, Mr. Pulliam, I appreciate your coming out and I hope you have a safe trip back. And gentlemen, it looks like we have our work cut out for us. We have to sell the company." It was so quiet you could hear the men's mouths drop open, then click shut. He turned to me saying, "Miss Beasley, you may buy the company under either method you have proposed." I'd made a fair offer and was getting a fair deal. A golden rule proposal had resulted in a gold rule result.

Consummating the sale took quite a while because their attorneys were reluctant to finalize the exact verbal agreement, but they finally did. We opened SAFECO Land Title of Dallas in 1979. Our chain of eight metroplex companies was completed in 1980 when my partners and I purchased a title plant in the remaining adjacent county.

Mr. Little of SAFECO Insurance has not been disappointed, nor have we. We've achieved all of our goals: being their top independent agent in the country since our first year, writing the greatest dollar volume of title business in Dallas county in 1984, writing more than any other independent agent in Texas in 1984. Reports for 1985, when filed, should show us on top again.

Besides my legal firm and title company involvement, I also own, in various partnerships, oil and gas interests, real estate, and several small manufacturing concerns. While I've achieved all I want materially, I don't plan to slack off, but to strive harder to continue achieving. There's always another challenge to be met.

TIPS FOR SUCCESS

1. Dream and have vision. Don't just focus on what's ahead but think what could be ahead.
2. Communicate your dreams and motivate others to make them theirs.
3. Be persistent, keep working; you may give out, but don't give up.
4. Create opportunities, take on a challenge, dare to risk a lot.
5. Be ethical and be of good character. Use your power wisely to follow the golden rule: "Do unto others what you would have them do unto you."
6. Share, show compassion, be willing to help others, and they'll help you; then reward all their efforts.
7. Enjoy your work and keep your sense of humor.
8. Have confidence in yourself and your courage, have faith.

> *"Faith is fear that has said its prayers.*
> *Faith is not contrary to reason:*
> *but rather, reason grown courageous."*

Elton Trueblood

"The sudden death of her husband thrust Helen Boehm into a position of enormous responsibility.**"**

Helen Boehm
Chairman
Edward Marshall Boehm, Inc.
Trenton, New Jersey

T here is nothing like success. I really cannot describe the feeling, but when it happens, you know it. My husband and I had a dream of making it in the world of porcelain and this is exactly what has happened. Why? Because from the beginning we were dedicated to excellence and to mirroring nature with fidelity—and we tried to improve every day. Our goal was to be the best and to provide the best.

The Work Ethic

I was born Elena Francesca Stefanie Franzolin into a family poor in money but very rich in love and happiness. My parents were Italian immigrants, and they taught their seven children the value and dignity of work. My father, a cabinet maker, died when I was quite young, and my mother became the head of the household. Because I was the youngest and at home more than my sisters and brothers my mother taught me not only how to cook, sew, and set a fine table but also to be useful with my hands—to do everything well. When my father died, my sisters and brothers and I had to take odd jobs to help out.

My earliest business success was as a dressmaker. As a teenager I made dresses for my friends and sold them for fifty cents each. I enjoyed using my hands to rip out the seams of a fabric, then sew it and match it to what they wanted. I was so good at designing and making dresses that I thought it would be my life's work—and I loved doing it.

After high school I got a job as a receptionist for our family's optometrist in Brooklyn. At night I took classes at the Mechanical School of Optics in Brooklyn Heights and studied optics and eye fashion. Soon I was one of the first women in New York licensed as a dispensing optician.

Becoming an Entrepreneur

At the age of twenty-four, I met my husband, Edward Boehm, who taught me that one could be a successful entrepreneur in many businesses. He introduced me to a wonderful new world of freedom. The freedom to take an opportunity, work hard, and succeed.

I had a strong drive to achieve and contribute and only needed an outlet within which to direct this drive. That opportunity came when Edward quit his job as assistant to a veterinarian. He wanted to be an artist and I wanted to help him. Ed worked day and night and eventually found the secret of making hard paste porcelain. Our next challenge was to create a market for Ed's sculptures—a market that would only buy European, English, or Asian porcelains.

My husband, an orphan, was a self-taught artist and a world-renowned aviculturist who had an intimate knowledge of birds and other animal species. I was a determined kid from Brooklyn with an eye for design and a strong sales talent. Together, we would produce and market the best in porcelain art objects. But at that time we were told it would take "one hundred years" to get Americans to consider Boehm porcelains over Minton, Worcester, Wedgwood, Spode, or Meissen.

Meeting the Challenge

When we began we had no collateral, nothing but our hands to show a bank. Twice the doors almost closed when we were on our own, and we came close to losing our one-room studio. Luckily, the First Mechanics Bank in Trenton, New Jersey, agreed to lend us $1,000 to keep going. After that, the bank manager continually would ask me, "Helen, did you sell something today?" and each time I would have to reply "No." Then the day came when I was able to tell him that we had sold some porcelains. What a relief! The pressure of paying back that one and only loan made me determined never again to borrow money from a bank.

Our first big break came in 1951 when I sold a "Percheron Stallion" and a "Hereford Bull" to the Metropolitan Museum of Art in New York City. They were Edward's first two porcelain sculptures. This gave Boehm the credibility that we needed to become one of the leaders in the field. That was in 1951 and the bull was listed at thirty dollars. Today a bull from this edition has sold for $4,800 at auction.

Now we are world leaders in fine porcelain. There is a sense and a feeling of reverence that one gets from picking up and studying a Boehm piece. It is not status—although to some it is—but I believe it is more than that. As Prince Charles said recently, "All that is missing from a Boehm rose is the fragrance." Until you hold one in your hand, you might not be able to tell the difference. When President Nixon took our famous porcelain "Birds of Peace," the "Mute Swans," to China with him in 1972, Mao Tse-Tung and the Chinese leaders asked, "Why is the president giving us stuffed birds?" There is a universal feeling that we are the best, that we can capture the reality of nature and freeze it permanently into porcelain.

Success Is Not Achieved between Nine and Five

If you are going to succeed as an entrepreneur you must have a product or service that you believe in with all your heart. You have to work at your craft day in and day out, many hours a day. One cannot expect a nine-to-five experience. That's not the way to get a new business started. Your work has to be primary in your life and with talent, knowledge, and faith in your product or service you can succeed. In the porcelain field, you have to be blessed with a variety of natural skills and talents that Edward Boehm had—a love of nature, the eyes and hands to render it in a fine medium, and the desire to be the best.

Our reputation is assured now but we had to earn it. We have worked hard for more than thirty years to get to this point. The world over people know the name Boehm in porcelain because we provide the best product. Talent plus tenacity, hard work, and the ability to motivate people have made the dream my husband and I shared possible.

My husband died in 1969, and my task was to carry on the great work he began. Since 1969 we have been recognized by china and porcelain experts the world over and, of course, Boehm porcelains are bought for their investment value as well as their beauty. In fact, in my Trenton studio there is a placard that reads, "Whatever is beautiful is also profitable."

Our next challenge will be to produce a collection of the human figure. We are primarily known for our flora, fauna, and fine art plates, but this will be the first time we are concentrating in an important way on the human figure.

Pride in Progress

Today when I see the progress women have made I feel immense pride because I understand what each one of us has gone through to achieve success. Frankly, I never felt discriminated against because of my sex—only because of an empty wallet. Perhaps I was too busy to recognize negative pressures. I never had the education of women I see entering the corporate world today, armed with college degrees and MBAs. They certainly are much better prepared. But to be an entrepreneur, to start one's own business, I believe that instinct, courage, determination, and a belief in the work ethic are equally important.

I have been told by chief executive officers of companies with whom I do business or on whose board I serve as a director that I am tough and demanding on matters regarding performance and holding down costs. That is praise I have earned through long experience and much trial and error. The trick is to keep the errors to a minimum. I also was not afraid to take risks. Business schools today stress the importance of risk taking. Of course you must take risks. Life is a collection of risks! You have to work to win. If you lose, you must work to win again. Entrepreneurship is both the most satisfying and the most exhausting activity there is in life.

Today there is still much hard work to be done. I have to help our company stay on top of the market. I travel constantly around the United States and abroad, alert, observing, and studying the market. Our studios must continue to grow and that means finding new skills and new forms of art with which to please Boehm collectors and patrons. When you achieve success in business, you don't just float at the top. You have to fight to stay at the top, and I welcome that fight.

TIPS FOR SUCCESS

1. Forget a nine-to-five schedule. If you want to be the best, you have to work as circumstances demand.
2. Time is valuable. Always be on time whenever you are making a presentation or showing something. Learn all there is to know about whom you are going to be talking to, and be clear, crisp, and concise.
3. Love what you are doing and show it. Enthusiasm sells!
4. Take risks. Even if you lose, you can always pick yourself up and move forward again. All of life is a collection of risks. You have to gamble to win.
5. Believe in teamwork, whether it is in your office, your studio, or your home. Do not be a prima donna. There is a reason that teams get to the top, and that is because they can work together.
6. Always be able to change your direction or your goals to meet changing times. If your original goal has become outdated, change it. No business goal or achievement is sacrosanct. If you stand still you'll atrophy.

"Masako Tani Boissonnault assimilated to a new culture with new customs, becoming successful alone, without the support of family or friends.**"**

Masako Tani Boissonnault
Principal, ARCH-I-FORM, Inc.
Los Angeles, California

I was born in Tokyo, Japan, in 1944, one year before the end of World War II. The war had been, and for the next decade would continue to be, a catalyst for change in Japan. Post-war Japan wanted to assimilate some of the ideas and concepts of western culture and I was raised during this rocky transition. I attribute many of my attitudes to being born at this turbulent period in history.

Education Encouraged

My father had a kimono business which he lost during the war and started up again with money borrowed from family and friends. I was the youngest of six children, four sisters and one brother. There were eight years between me and the next youngest and fourteen years between me and the oldest sister. My parents worked very hard to support the family, and the children were expected to help our parents with the kimono business.

My father was unable to complete his formal schooling but he provided each of his children with the opportunities and tools to get a good education. My mother encouraged me to study drawing, piano, and dancing while attending elementary school, and much of my youth was spent studying and working. I respected my father's wishes and studied hard to please him in spite of the fact that he would periodically remind me "the smartest woman is equal to the dumbest man."

When I was thirteen, my mother died. This event forced me to become more independent and self-sufficient at the same time I was supposed to take on the care of my father. Japanese tradition dictates that the oldest son goes into the family business. My brother was an architect, and didn't want to go into the kimono business, but when my mother passed away, he had no choice. Later, he and the others tried to get me to go into the business, but I refused. I had other goals in mind.

By the time I reached high school, all of my sisters had married. Their futures would focus on caring for their home, their children, their husband, and their husband's father. I wanted something different, something better, and I realized that this meant leaving Japan. Even though economic and social changes were being made in Japan, traditions and roles were strongly entrenched.

Career Dreams

I began dreaming of a career, of traveling around the world, of being totally independent. My first goal was to become a top-notch commercial designer. To this end, I enrolled at Tama Fine Art College in Japan where I graduated with a Bachelor of Fine Arts degree.

My second goal was to continue my education at the famous Art Center College of Design in Los Angeles, California. But first I had to learn English.

After studying English for one and a half years, I applied to the Art Center College of Design and was immediately accepted. My dream was becoming a reality. A final step was to gain the approval and support from my father and sisters and brother. This became a real lesson in the art of persuasion and negotiation. In 1969, I began my studies.

It was a dream come true, but it was tough. A year and a half of English did not prepare me for postgraduate studies. But I studied hard because I knew that if I gave up I would have to go back to Japan.

In 1973, I joined the Japanese firm of Kajima Associates in Los Angeles as a designer. Through this association I acquired direct experience in commercial design for banks, restaurants, offices, hotels, and manufacturing facilities. With experience and success came larger and more complex projects.

A Design Consultant

After four and a half years, I decided to establish myself as a design consultant. My primary clients were two small architectural firms with Japanese employees and Japanese clients. My confidence was increasing. After another year I decided it was time to break out of this mold.

Another goal emerged. I wanted to prove myself and work for a recognized and successful American design firm. My design skills were good and I had gained confidence in my abilities, but I wanted to be recognized and successful with American business people.

I joined the firm of Timothy H. Walker in 1977. New opportunities emerged to refine my skills and techniques, including new ways of arranging space and forms. I also had the opportunity to learn many aspects of running a design business, including marketing, public relations, and sales.

My goal was to be recognized for my capability and talent. This required diligence, discipline, and hard work. I wanted to finish my projects ahead of schedule so I could be assigned to new ones. The hard work paid off. I gained the respect and commendation of my peers.

Starting My Own Business

In 1980, my husband, Neil Boissonnault, whom I had married while a student, encouraged me to go out on my own. I decided to join a colleague and form our own commercial design firm, ARCH-I-FORM, Inc. I borrowed $5,000 from a personal friend to capitalize the business. We started out with good ideas, very little money, and no clients.

It took six months to get ARCH-I-FORM established. Our first break was when the Carte Blanche credit card company retained us to remodel its headquarters. On completion of this project, I was able to fully repay the money I had borrowed to finance the business. Over the past five years, ARCH-I-FORM has done work for such clients as Diner's Club, TRW, Candle Corporation, and numerous branch banks, offices, and restaurants.

Part of having your own business is becoming involved in the community. In 1983, I also taught advanced interior space planning at Woodbury University. I have been active in the American Business Women's Assocation's local chapter. In 1984, I was selected as one of the Top Ten Business Women of the year. I participated in the National Association of Owners and the Society and Marketing Professional Services. And I have a daily regimen dedicated to exercise for good mental and physical health.

For the future, my partner and I intend to establish a business plan which will build our client base, expand our services to capture a broader client base, and perhaps design and build our own commercial building.

Very early in life I recognized what I wanted and did not want. Some of this may have been circumstantial, but without determination, discipline, tenacity, and a willingness to take risks, I never would have come to this country.

Life in a New Country

My story may seem unique because I left my family to come to the United States to study. I had to learn a new language and to learn to think like an American. This meant assimilating a new culture and new customs. How could I fail when I was surrounded by people who had a "can do" attitude about business and life? As a newcomer to this country I could truly appreciate the incredible opportunity the free enterprise system provides not only for women but for all citizens. The range of opportunity and choices available to everyone was confusing to me at first, but gradually I developed a stronger sense of my own identity and culture—enhanced by the culture of my new country.

When you are forced to survive on your own, without family or friends, you learn very quickly what your strengths and weaknesses are and you learn to become comfortable with yourself. This is an ongoing challenge.

I believe that patience is an absolute necessity for achievement. Success takes time and you must keep your eye on your goal through daily failures, roadblocks, and detours. There is no short cut. Minimize your failures because sometimes they become the steppingstones to eventual success.

TIPS FOR SUCCESS

1. Try to identify in the larger sense what you want for yourself and go for it.
2. Don't be afraid of failure and don't be afraid to take risks.
3. Try to adopt habits that will facilitate the achievement of your goals.
4. Always try to keep at least one goal in front of you.
5. Set your goals early and do all that you can to achieve them.
6. Have a daily regimen dedicated to exercise for good mental and physical health.

"Dale Hanson Bourke broke the tedious mold of routine office work to discover the secret to being a creative professional.**"**

Dale Hanson Bourke
President,
Publishing Directions, Inc.
Washington, D.C.

I know there are people who don't like to work, but I am not one of them. From my earliest, most boring, most repetitive tasks through today's more exciting and diverse roles, I have always loved the work itself. In many ways I don't think it would have mattered to me if I'd ended up in publishing or in construction. I love the work. I love seeing something accomplished. I love making things happen.

The "Entrepreneurial Oath."

My husband jokes that I must have taken the entrepreneurial equivalent of the Hippocratic oath. Just as a doctor can't pass an accident without helping a victim, I can't pass by an opportunity without trying to make it into a success. We could be eating dinner in a quiet restaurant and I'll begin sizing up ways to increase the business. We might be relaxing on a beach and I'll begin to invent concessions that could do well. It's not that I'm just a dreamer. If my husband didn't temper my tendencies at times, I'd be talking to the manager about buying the restaurant or getting a permit to become a beach vendor. I really like making things happen and I'm not afraid of the hard work that turns ideas into success stories.

Perhaps that's why I don't really fear failure. I'm almost intrigued by the idea of starting over; I like to watch a checkout clerk at the supermarket or a waitress in a restaurant and wonder what it would be like to do those jobs again. I know I'm not too proud to do any job and I'm grateful that I have never believed that I would rise above a certain type of work. To me, there can be joy and a sense of accomplishment in any job.

I suppose I am a bit of a crusader on the subject of enjoying one's job. I think anyone can love what they do and I don't believe there's any excuse for not doing the very best job possible. Whenever I see someone shuffling through a job or moping I think about all the energy that person is wasting on negative thoughts and self-pity. It's so much more draining to suffer through a job than to throw yourself into it wholeheartedly.

It probably sounds as if it's easy for me to talk about loving one's job. I have my own company, my work is diverse and exciting, and I travel regularly. Wouldn't anyone love her work if she had a life like mine? Maybe. There are still the tough choices that only I make and live with, the shuffling of priorities and the balancing act that threatens my sanity some days, the lonely nights in hotel rooms when I'd give anything to be home with my family. Those are some of the costs of my job. But in many ways this isn't any different from the other jobs I've had. There were always trade-offs.

Selling Door to Door

My very first job was selling packages of seeds door to door in my home town in Illinois. With the promise of "bonus points for every package sold" looming in my eight-year-old head, I canvassed the neighborhood. I soon discovered that even with the kind generosity of my neighbors, I'd never accumulate enough points to win more than a dimestore toy. Disappointed, but not discouraged, I moved on to selling Girl Scout cookies and soon fell in love with the thrill of the sale.

By the time I was a teenager I had acquired typing skills and a strong desire to work, so my father let me help out at his office during summers. I soon discovered the boredom of clerical work: hours of filing forms, copying reams of paper, typing invoices. I watched the clock and prayed to make it until the next break. Every work day seemed to last forever.

A Change In Attitude

Then I began to read books by Norman Vincent Peale and Dale Carnegie. I was introduced to the idea of having a positive mental attitude. I began to try it at the office, I stopped complaining at coffee breaks, I began to smile and give a cheerful word to anyone I dealt with, and I began to play games with every task. I'd see how many forms I could file in an hour and then try to beat my record. I'd develop faster ways to copy materials. It sounds silly, but it worked. I actually began to like what I did, and, of course, my supervisors loved my attitude and productivity. When I think about it, that may have been the turning point in my career. If I'd continued to suffer through work I might be an unhappy clerk to this day. But I vowed to work hard and enjoy everything I did and that attitude separated me from others time and time again.

While in high school I took a journalism class and fell in love with the printed word. I became editor of the high school newspaper and learned about everything from typesetting to proofreading to selling advertising. It was one of the best experiences of my teenage years and gave me a wonderful glimpse of the world of publishing. I dreamed of working for *Time* magazine someday.

Major Influences

The major influences at that point in my life were my parents. They had a practical, midwestern view of life and instilled the principles of hard work in me from the start. But they also encouraged me to stretch for whatever I wanted and helped me believe that I could do or be anything if I wanted to badly enough.

My father is a businessman who is always trying to find ways to do things better. So when Peter Drucker's *Management by Objectives* was published in the late sixties, my father not only read it and began to apply it at work, but he also brought its principles home. As a teenager I was encouraged to set clear objectives and to work toward them. When I look back, it seems clear that the discipline imposed on my thinking as a teenager was a very important key to my career success. Although I was influenced by the attitudes of the late sixties and early seventies, I was generally more purposeful than my teenage counterparts. By the time I was ready for college I had already begun to set life goals.

I considered going to a large state university where I could major in journalism, but decided instead to go to Wheaton College, a small private college with an excellent English department. At Wheaton I began to work on the student newspaper during the first week of school. But the student newspaper was strictly volunteer work, so I also began to look for other jobs on campus. Being a freshman, my options were limited to the serving line in the student cafeteria. It was a greasy job and it was hot standing over the steaming trays of food. But remembering my vow to enjoy whatever I did, I decided to make it more fun by arranging everyone's food in interesting shapes and patterns (long before nouvelle cuisine). Soon the job seemed like fun and students coming through the line would talk and joke with me, making the time go quickly.

My college was in a wealthy suburb of Chicago and many women employed college girls for housecleaning. The idea of making $20 for a day of housecleaning was very appealing, so in addition to my cafeteria job, I signed up to clean houses two days a week. All of my working hours plus a full class schedule and a freshman's social life meant that I simply had no time for sleep. By the second quarter of my freshman year I was in bed to stay with mononucleosis. I think that God may have been showing me early on that my workaholic tendencies would have to be curbed if I was to lead a balanced life. After recovering I cut back to one job at a time—at least for a while.

First Editorial Job

By the time I was a junior in college I had become editor of the college newspaper. It was a more difficult job than I think I've ever had—producing a weekly newspaper with an entirely volunteer staff. After my work on the newspaper I became a writer for the college public relations office. Through that office I received information about the Public Relations Society of America and its summer student internship program. I filled out the application and was thrilled to be selected for one of the positions at a trade association preparing for a major industry convention. I went from being a college student to being a downtown commuter with an office in Chicago's Loop and the prestige of a professional position. It was the first time I had ever worked in an office without being the lowest person on the totem pole, and I didn't even have to psych myself up for the job—I loved it.

I enjoyed the job so much that when school started in the fall I continued to work downtown two days a week and be a college student the rest of the time. Although I still enjoyed school and made good grades, I knew that my heart belonged in the working world. I could hardly wait to start my first full-time job.

A month before graduation I had two job offers: one with a prestigious public relations firm in Chicago, near my family and friends, the other with a small association in Washington, D.C., where I knew no one. It was at that point that I established another pattern that I have often followed throughout my career—I chose the underdog. I moved to Washington because I knew I'd be a big fish in a small organization. And there was something frightening about staying in Chicago where my life was so secure. I wanted to see the rest of the world and I was afraid that if I stayed in Chicago I'd be there for the rest of my life. I needed to stretch if I was to grow.

The Move to Washington, D.C.

In Washington I was publications director of the Christian College Consortium, an education association of small private colleges. I was a one-person publications office. I edited and produced a small magazine and later started a syndicated news service. I was the editor of the newly established university press; I wrote press releases, brochures, and anything else that needed to come out of our headquarters. It was an overwhelming job at first, but I loved its diversity and the fact that I was working in the field of my choice.

My boss was a hard worker and very goal-oriented. He picked up where my father left off with a very organized management by objectives approach. Although it often seemed that I had more objectives than hours in the day, I learned to work at a fast pace and differentiate quickly the urgent from the important. Seeing so much of my work in print was extremely gratifying and gave me a continuing sense of accomplishment.

When the association began to work on a cooperative marketing program for its member colleges, it seemed natural that I would help work on the promotion materials. Although I had always loved writing I was often bothered by the lack of measurable objectives in journalism. In promotional writing I found the perfect fit between my desire to communicate and my objective orientation. I became totally enamored with marketing and began to work on the association's program with great interest.

We had hired an outside consulting firm to direct our marketing efforts and I found myself getting a free internship in a new field by working with the consultants. To this day, I have learned to hire consultants whenever I am trying to solve a problem outside of my area of experience. Not only do I avoid serious mistakes because of my lack of knowledge, but I also have the opportunity to learn a new area from the perspective of an expert.

Realizing then that marketing was more than a passing interest, I decided to pursue an MBA. But I couldn't afford to go to school full-time and I also knew that I'd never be happy as a full-time student. I needed to stay involved in the real world of work. So I began to take classes in the evenings and work full-time during the day. It was a grueling schedule for two and a half years, but by the end of 1978 I had an MBA and a much clearer understanding of the business world.

Beginning a Marketing Career

Before I finished my degree I went to work for the marketing consultant firm as a copywriter and account assistant. Within a year I had my first account to direct on my own. I loved working with clients. It blended all of the joys of sales and helping people with the desire to set objectives and see them realized. I also began to travel more often and even came to enjoy the bustle of balancing airline schedules and hotel reservations.

In the meantime I met and married my husband, a busy architect with the patience to accept my schedule, the sense of humor to deal with the stress of my job, and the confidence not only to support me in my career, but also to push me to be all I could be. I cannot think of a time when Tom has done anything other than encourage me in my work. I know many women feel torn between their home life and their career, and I feel the strain at times too, but it's never because my husband adds pressure.

After working for the marketing firm for two years, one of the partners I often worked with decided to start a company of his own. He asked me to start it with him and made me vice-president. We were almost frantically busy from our first day with a growing list of clients and expanding services and no time even to interview new staff members. It was thrilling as well as exhausting and the pace never seemed to slow for the next three years.

Developing a Reputation

We developed a strong reputation for direct mail as well as market research and specialized in work for nonprofit organizations. The most exciting aspect of our work was to see the difference it made to charitable organizations that often needed professional help in order to accomplish their purposes. Not only did I enjoy the work, but I also gained great satisfaction from helping important causes and showing them how to be more efficient in fund raising.

My sense of never letting an opportunity pass me by led me to help expand the firm into the areas of public relations and publishing. Many of the organizations we worked with desperately needed help in their total communications programs. We began to give them assistance with press relations and even began to help them improve their magazines.

If our firm had any problem it was unguided success. We were simply doing too much in too many areas. Quality began to suffer, our staff was exhausted, and we began to feel that we were simply turning things out without thought. The one thing I realized would undermine my job satisfaction was feeling that I wasn't doing my best. I became frustrated that there was never enough time to do a good job. Eventually my frustration led to a proposal to the president that we split the company by areas of expertise. After many talks it became clear that setting up divisions of the company was less feasible than simply splitting off areas. At that point I decided to buy the contracts of clients for which we were producing magazines. It was the newest part of the company and the area in which I was most comfortable and qualified.

Starting Publishing Directions

In October of 1981 I formed Publishing Directions as a consulting and publishing firm. We had three clients, quaint offices, used furniture, and a very modest bank account. But I was the president and I could dream, risk, and even fail with no one to blame but myself. It was a frightening but thrilling beginning to what has been a real adventure.

Publishing Directions has enjoyed success over the past four years primarily, I believe, because we give our clients more than they expect. We always go the extra mile. We care about them. They come to trust us and give us a great deal of freedom to represent them. I also hire people who are committed to excellence in what they do. I want people to be happy with their work and proud of what they produce.

As company president, I'm also very careful to contain the overhead costs and keep our fixed expenses from controlling us. I've seen too many small firms desperately trying to cover a high rent after losing an account. I never want to be in a position where we can't afford to lose an account.

I love what I do. I wake up each morning excited about going to the office and facing the challenges of another day. The only difficulty I really face is when I leave my two-year-old son behind as I go on a business trip or when I leave for the office early and miss my good morning hug. But having my own company gives me the flexibility to bring him with me on occasion or to spend some mornings working at home. I'm grateful that I've enjoyed some measure of success in my career which enables me to have more freedom and flexibility.

It's important to me to keep my priorities straight. I do love work, but it isn't—or shouldn't be—the most important thing in my life. Every now and then it seems that God puts something in my path to remind me of those possibilities. Sometimes it's a small reminder—a missed airplane that gives me more time with my family. Sometimes it's more major—a failed acquisition attempt that teaches me the importance of humility. Although it's easy to find great satisfaction in work, it's important to maintain my value system. God, my family, and others as well need to come before my job. Success often seems to be measured by salaries or titles. But I learned very early in my career that true success is experiencing inner peace and happiness.

TIPS FOR SUCCESS

1. Have a positive attitude. Get excited about your work. Look for positives in it and the people you deal with each day. Make a point to be pleasant, upbeat, and responsive.

2. Set clear objectives. It's vitally important to have clear long-term goals as well as shorter-term objectives to help you attain your goals. Even if you don't always reach the mark, you subliminally concentrate on that long-term goal and channel your energy in the proper direction.

3. Don't be greedy. Too many people in business try to make a quick dollar and then lose a great long-term deal. It's never worth it to risk a friendship or a potential business contract in order to profit in the short term.

4. Be confident but not proud. Everybody loves a winner and wants to feel that their trust is well placed in you. But confidence should never be confused with pride or an unwillingness to do anything to get the job done properly.

5. Never stop risking, stretching, and dreaming. No one can afford to feel settled or static in a job. Whenever you stop trying to do the very best you can you lose a bit of your professional range. Allow yourself to compromise. If you're not growing in your job, find ways to improvise or find a new job.

"Barbara Capsalis had to sort out the conflict between her drive for personal perfection and the need to be a team player.**"**

Barbara Capsalis
Senior Vice-President,
Chemical Bank of New York
New York, New York

W hen I entered college in the 1960s, I expected to graduate, work one or two years, get married, and live happily ever after in a lovely suburban home, with two children, two cars, nice clothes, and summer and winter vacations each year. In fact, my adult life began just that way—I married right after college and started working.

Twenty years later I am still married and still working. As a senior vice-president at the Chemical Bank in New York, I am responsible for the bank's non-credit services worldwide. I have a job scope and level that in my industry is generally held by men. I manage 2,500 people, performing marketing and sales, technical and operational activities. I am at the senior most level held by women in the bank.

I have always thought that the key to whatever success I enjoy can be credited to being in the right place at the right time. My right place was data processing. It was something I did very well and my performance was rewarded with increases in responsibility. Getting to the "right place" took some doing. Each responsibility I accepted prepared me to move closer to my goal— opportunities in general management.

Enjoying the Intellectual Challenge

Part of my success process was learning that I really enjoyed the intellectual challenges of working. I liked the feeling of accomplishment and personal pride that comes from doing things well. Of course there is a financial reward but the psychic reward is just as important. Concurrently, my husband and I learned how nice it could be for each of us to have individual careers and to build a life together.

What happened to change the opportunities and aspirations of American women like me? Several important things. During the last two decades, the political, economic, and social fabric surrounding the American free enterprise system have enabled American women to become full participants. Affirmative action legislation requiring that women and men be treated equally in entry and promotional policy insured full access to the free enterprise system. The combination of general inflation and the economic recession of the mid-1970s made a second income mandatory for some families, and at least desirable for others. It became economically desirable and socially acceptable for women to have a job.

Growth in the general economy and the relatively greater growth rate in the service sector made entry and promotion easier for women than it might have been during a period of economic decline, or during a period of relatively larger growth rate in more tradition bound sectors, such as manufacturing or agriculture.

The Legacy of the Recent Past

The legacy of these last decades is (1) a free enterprise system that enables and supports parity of women in the work place, (2) an educational system that prepares us for participation, and (3) a cultural environment in which freedom of choice for women and the two-career family are the norm.

Whether you are entrepreneuring with your own business or intrapreneuring as part of a corporation, it is important to know yourself. In fact, I wish I knew twenty years ago what would make me happy today so I could have done more then. I also wish I knew today what will make me happy twenty years from now. But I've always known certain things about myself and that knowledge has helped me make decisions along the way. I like analytic problem solving, so I majored in mathematics at a time when women math majors were few and far between. I like working with people more than just solving purely technical problems. That helped me choose general management rather than a purely technical career path.

What I also know about myself is that I have a need to aim for perfection. I also know that this drive for perfection can create problems. As a young woman, starting out in the business world, I had to learn to be more flexible, a little less of the perfectionist and more of a team player.

I made a lot of mistakes trying to figure out if the roadblocks I thought were in my way were the result of organizational politics—or my own high expectations of myself and others. The answer to this question was so important to me that I took a year and a half off and worked for the city of New York in order to look more closely at organizational politics in action. What I learned was that it was not politics holding me back but my attitude.

A Humbling Experience

It was a humbling experience but I realized I needed to listen to others more, to be less critical, to encourage open discussion of ideas, to work more as a team player. Did I make mistakes? I certainly did, but I tried not to make the same one twice.

Throughout your career you will be faced with choices: Should I take this new assignment? Should I change jobs? Along the way you learn to trust your instincts in making decisions. If it feels right, I'll do it; if it doesn't feel right, I'll pass. The corollary to that is not to belly ache. If you made a poor choice, make another. If you feel that you are underpaid or under-recognized for your work, don't complain, find a new job.

Although education alone will not guarantee success, I have always been glad that I had a good education. The increasing competition in the free enterprise system requires the highest caliber of performance, and a good education is frequently the ticket of entry to the corporate world. Once you're admitted you must continue to stay up to date in your field; keep learning.

Greater Opportunities and Challenges for Women

There are new barriers and new challenges for women today because the economic environment is more competitive and more internationalized than ever before. The challenge to the American free enterprise system is to continue its growth through intelligent emphasis on those sectors of the economy where we have a competitive advantage while minimizing the dislocations caused by de-emphasis of those in which we cannot compete effectively.

This argues that women entering the work place for the first time will have greater opportunities in service- and technology-related industries. It also argues for specialized education or re-education for women in unskilled manufacturing and clerical positions which can be performed more economically abroad.

The demographic composition of our population is changing also. One example of this is the migration of jobs from the northeast and midwest, indicating that entry and promotional opportunities may be better in some parts of the country than others. A second example of potential change is the glut of new workers resulting from the combination of the higher birth rate of the post-war baby boom generation and the large numbers of women entering or re-entering the market. This implies that the rapid advancement achieved by my generation may not continue, and that the reward structure may change.

The intellectual stimulation I found from increased responsibilities might be achieved by moving to different jobs at the same level. The financial rewards might require changing companies or entrepreneurial ventures, rather than spending a lifetime with one company.

The good news is that women today start out equal to men as they enter the free enterprise system; the challenge is to know what you want from it and then figure out how to get it.

Women are becoming policy makers even in major corporations and exciting opportunities are opening up daily. Even the traditionally male-dominated industries now have "sexless" entry requirements and promotional parity through upper middle management levels. Within the American free enterprise system, there are myriad opportunities to feel good about yourself and to enjoy your life. Decide what it is you like to do, get the proper education, seek each day to do the best job you are capable of doing, and the rewards will be there.

TIPS FOR SUCCESS

1. March to your own drummer. Recognize certain things about yourself that can allow you to do better in everything you do.

2. Get a good education and continue it. A good education is the price of admission into any sort of career advancement.

3. Work hard and have high integrity. I am constantly amazed at the amount of time young people spend on organizational politics and worrying about their careers rather than on doing a first-class job on their particular assignment. Perceptions may count in the short term, but substance always prevails. Second, set a high personal standard about how you do business and stick to it. Compromising your principles may gain you a friend or some money in the short run, but respect earns you the longer-term opportunities and gains.

4. Don't be averse to risks. Be willing to take a chance. Throughout your career you will be faced with choices. Don't always take the easy one. Try to do something that may be a little more difficult because the rewards will be that much better.

5. Balance your personal and professional lives. Perhaps the most rewarding part of my life is the fact that I have both a good career and a good marriage. When a disappointment occurs in one area, I have the other to fall back on. Keeping that balance does not come easily, and if you take one aspect for granted for too long, you will lose it.

6. Have fun and be happy. Decide what it is you like to do, get the proper education, seek each day to do the best job you are capable of doing, and the rewards will be there for you too!

"A foreigner and a woman, Tatiana Brandt Copeland chose to compete in the male world of international tax and finance. She is now a tax CPA and financial planner for multi-million dollar clients.**"**

Tatiana Brandt Copeland
President,
Tebec Associates Limited
Wilmington, Delaware

I have been on the move from the very beginning of my life, aware that risk and uncertainty were a normal part of my environment. My family, part of the Russian aristocracy, was forced to flee Russia after the Revolution and decided to settle in Dresden, East Germany, where they owned some property. After World War II (just after I was born in Dresden), we were again forced to flee from East Germany because of the Communists, and this time settled in Denmark. In our haste to escape, we left everything behind and arrived in Copenhagen with little more than the clothes on our back and a few precious mementos. After a couple of years in Denmark, we moved to Argentina, where I did most of my growing up. If change at an early age is a requirement for a successful entrepreneur, I certainly qualify! At this point, English was my fifth language and the toughest one to learn, but I was speaking it fluently by the time I came to study in the United States at UCLA. However, I still felt more at home with Russian, Spanish, French, and German!

Parental Influence

I can't speak for other women entrepreneurs, but the greatest influence in my life, encouraging me to take risks, to be confident, to work hard and have a positive attitude, were my parents. Although they lost everything (several times over), they had not lost their spirit or zest for life and they were supportive of anything I expressed interest in doing. This was unusual because my formative years were spent in the traditional environment of South America where women's roles are clearly delineated. It never occurred to them, or to me, that I couldn't do something simply because I was a girl. In fact, I was always pushed and encouraged to do better.

Quite honestly, I never could have achieved what I have today in any other country but this one. America has been absolutely amazing to me. Being a foreigner was tough enough—but a foreign-born woman faces double obstacles. The difference in this country, and one that most native-born Americans cannot realize, is that the U.S. offers opportunities to those who are willing and able to work, and work hard. I can't say that it wasn't difficult at times, but at least I believed that success could be achieved if I was willing to work long and hard enough.

Even with all the hard work and many roadblocks, I think I've been unusually lucky. I've established a strong professional reputation in a field dominated by men. When I started, there just weren't that many women in the financial field because dealing with money and power were not viewed as traditional or appropriate goals for women. When I graduated from UCLA's School of Business, out of a graduating class of 500, only two were women (the top two of the class, if I remember correctly!).There was no mentor to guide or advise me, and certainly no female professional I could turn to.

A Lone Fish in a Big Pond

There's always a risk when you are the "first" in any profession. I often felt as if I were under a microscope being analyzed and evaluated constantly. I was a woman doing a job that had never been done by a woman before—a lone fish in a very big pond. Discrimination wasn't overt but it was there.

Before I had my own business, I worked for Price Waterhouse, Whittaker Corporation, and DuPont. I believed that because they had been in business a long time, with established reputations, they could offer me the best opportunities to grow and develop. It was also true that these companies were often led by people—especially those in middle management—who had mixed feelings about women climbing to the top of the corporate ladder. But I was young and refused to think that opportunity would be denied just because I was a woman. Incomprehensible!

Realities of the Corporate World

When I interviewed with the DuPont Company I was offered a job in their European headquarters, at Geneva, Switzerland, which was the reason I accepted the offer. Geneva is viewed as a choice assignment and there were many of my peers who felt I had not worked long enough within the company to receive such a "plum" job. I shortly became aware that my assignment had ruffled quite a few feathers, both by my being new to the company and a woman. My answer to criticism of this kind was to try to work harder, to make sure that my contribution to the company would be positive. I do believe performance can overcome prejudice and preconceptions to a certain degree. Early in my working career, I quickly learned that one of the realities of the corporate world is that women have to work harder than men to achieve the same level of respect. I was not afraid of hard work but there comes a point when you must move on to another job or another company if no matter how hard you work or how good your work is, you simply are never going to be taken seriously or because of an intangible feeling (by your boss) that a woman simply should not reach a higher position.

At this point in my career, as the president of my own company, those days are behind me and I no longer have to deal with overt prejudice. The clients who choose me feel comfortable having a woman deal with their financial affairs because they are satisfied with my performance.

I am an overachiever and a perfectionist. I find it difficult to accept the possibility of failure, although I obviously know it exists. I want to be the best and am constantly striving to reach higher goals for myself. I do not measure my performance against others but against myself. What did I accomplish this year as opposed to last year? What have I learned this year? How have I grown? I have never said to myself "I wish I could" because if I wish it then I do it. This is perhaps something one can't explain. A wish is part of the road that leads to a goal, and once you deal with goals you can decide how to make that wish come true.

Because my life has been filled with dramatic changes I try to be flexible and view change as a friend, not an enemy to be feared. I think this is a valuable attitude because you keep your thinking and creativity fresh—and you take absolutely nothing and no one for granted.

Roadblocks As Ladders

It is interesting to me that so many of my worst roadblocks turned out to be my ladders to success, pushing me to open my own firm and leaving the safe corporate world behind. Starting a business was something I always longed to do. I just never realized it could be as fulfilling as it turned out to be. I was especially fortunate because my husband, who had his own successful career, was very supportive. He also gave me something very special—the possibility to take chances without endangering the economic life of the family. His faith in me also took away my fear of failing. In fact, I felt that not trying would be a more profound failure than trying and failing. I will forever be grateful for his encouragement—the right push at the right time. As a result, I've been less afraid to take risks or chances. I have succeeded; I could just as easily have failed.

It's very difficult for someone—man or woman—to start their own business. Usually, people make one of two mistakes: they don't have enough starting capital or they don't have enough organizational talent. A business that starts out of someone's dream or vision or invention must have sufficient capital and administrative skills to make it a success.

Helping Fellow Entrepreneurs

It is important for every new entrepreneur to know that everyone, even the most successful businessperson, experiences frustrations. While I was still climbing the corporate ladder I belonged to several groups such as the American Society of Women Accountants and Wilmington Women in Business. At that time, I thought my feelings of frustration with my career were rather unique. After talking to my fellow group members,

I realized that many other women in business were facing the same type of problems, and this somehow made me feel better.

Today I'm in a position to help other women and this is very important to me. I believe that women should help one another and I practice this belief in my own business—my staff is all female. I try to keep active in professional business organizations for women in order to keep current about what is happening "out there." Networking groups can help the female entrepreneur; through the exchange of information you can get a better idea of what your product or service is worth on the open market. Women frequently complain that they are underpaid. One obvious reason is discrimination—women doing the same job often earn less than their male colleagues. But is it also because the female entrepreneur asks for less than her male counterpart? Interestingly enough, although I have encountered my fair share of discrimination, I have never been underpaid for my work. My professional counsel is the result of long and arduous training and it is neither free nor cheap.

Defining Success

My attitude toward success is realistic. I don't think I've "made it" and I hope I never think in those terms. There are so many things I still want to accomplish in my life. It would be a terrible thing to think that there are no more mountains to climb, no more goals to achieve, that success means resting on a plateau for the remainder of one's life. Success is a funny word. I used to think that success was one's reputation, being the best or among the best at what you do, and having the freedom and strength of character to do what you want. I now think that to be truly successful, I must achieve a greater balance between my personal and professional lives. Right now my life is definitely not balanced. I have this tug-of-war going on, trying to be a wife, a hostess, a career woman, and part of me wants to cave in. My goal in the next two years is to reach that elusive inner balance.

I truly enjoy what I do and thrive on the ups and downs, variety and pressures of being an entrepreneur. I'm a happy workaholic. I work long hours, but I love what I do and I have fun with it. I thrive on variety—in life, in work, in food, in travel—and love working on many projects. There is just one thing I might add to my life, and that's political involvement. I'm appalled at the number of people I meet (usually middle management men!) who simply don't seem to like what they're doing. Life is worthwhile and exciting when it's filled with challenges and new goals—after all, you only have one life to live!

TIPS FOR SUCCESS

1. Probably the hardest thing is to figure out exactly what you want to do in life—and then do it.
2. Have a dream and a desire to succeed, an inner driving force to ever reach higher.
3. Work hard. Success is a strenuous activity.
4. This may sound a bit simplistic, but always do a little more and a little better than is required. Go the extra mile. (Most people don't!) Doing everything you're told to do is not enough.
5. Listen to your intuitive self. Take time to nurture yourself. Create an environment where you can occasionaly remove yourself from daily problems and do some good thinking about the future.
6. Have someone important in your life (a husband, a friend, or a family member) who is totally supportive of you.
7. Find a good mentor.
8. Be determined and be professional.
9. Find the best people you can to assist you in your work.
10. And finally, have a "wife" at home to take care of all the important details in your life to free you to tackle the larger goals!

"Mary C. Crowley, through faith and hard work, recognized opportunities where others saw none and built a $350 million business."

Mary C. Crowley
President,
Home Interiors and Gifts, Inc.
Dallas, Texas

M y childhood was filled with change beginning at an early age. My mother died when I was eighteen months old and my grandparents became my parents. They gave me a warm, loving home and a strong foundation based on the fact that God's love could conquer any situation. When I was six years old my father remarried and told my grandparents that he wanted me to live with him and his new wife. It was with a heavy heart that I left my grandparents' home in Kansas and rode the train to begin a new life in Washington State.

Good Advice

I missed my grandparents and wanted to return to their love and wisdom. When I was thirteen, the juvenile court declared my stepmother unfit and I went back to them. With my grandmother's help I overcame the resentment I felt for my stepmother. Grandmother told me, "Every tub must sit on its own bottom. Don't live in if only land."

This was important advice that I would need to remember through the hard times of the Depression years. Married and a mother right after high school, I quickly learned that I would have to be the provider for my children—my husband was not ready for family responsibilities. I took in sewing and baked bread, using the money to buy food.

At the age of twenty-one I knew it would be necessary for me to work full-time. These were the Depression years and the entire country was out of work. There were no jobs available anywhere. How did I get one? By showing my potential employer how he would benefit by hiring me—benefit without a risk. I told the owner of our town's largest department store that I could bring in enough sales to pay my salary. He decided to try me for one day only—a Saturday. A standard custom in those days was to price things three cents less than the dollar. This meant that a customer would have to wait, after a purchase was made and the money was sent up to the office on a conveyer belt, for her three cents change to come back. I convinced customers that for only one penny more they could buy a spool of thread and be on their way. At the end of my first day the spool racks of thread were almost empty. The customers loved the idea. My temporary job became permanent and I was on my way, loving my work and helping my family.

Continuing an Education

My next goal was to continue my education so that I could qualify for a better job. I was good in math and knew if I could go to business school I could start to qualify as a CPA. The challenge was to find the money not only to attend but to travel back and forth to Dallas—a hundred miles away. The money came to me in the form of a $100 scholarship from the Rotary Club. This was an annual award given to a deserving student. This award was very special to me because at the time I was not a student, but they felt I should receive it anyway. I enrolled in business school and commuted back and forth between Dallas and Sherman. Eventually, when I could afford it, after my marriage ended, I moved to Dallas with my children and went to work for an insurance company.

My early experiences taught me that there is always opportunity, even in the worst of times. There will always be times when things are not just the way you want them but there is always a way to get past roadblocks. What does a roadblock tell you? That the road continues on the other side.

A Code of Ethics

When I started Home Interiors and Gifts, Inc., I wanted to have a company that would help other women deal with their roadblocks of insecurity, fear, lack of self-confidence, poverty. I built the business on a code of ethics that said:

> We believe in the dignity and importance of women.
>
> We believe that everything women touch should be ennobled by that touch.
>
> We believe that the home is the greatest influence on the character of mankind.
>
> We believe that the home should be a haven—a place of refuge, a place of peace, a place of harmony, a place of beauty.
>
> No home in America ever need be dull and unattractive.
>
> We are dedicated to doing our part to make every home have Attraction Power.

Our salesforce was all women, most of whom had never worked before or received college degrees. But by working together not only did Home Interiors thrive but our sales force grew in confidence and personal self-esteem as well. Several years ago, I took a poll of the thousands of women who were attending Home Interiors' rallies across the country. I wanted to know what each woman thought she wanted more of in the key areas of her life: home and family, business and career, community and social life. The one trait all of these women wanted most was a better self-image and a greater feeling of self-confidence. I was determined to help each woman with whom I came in contact to think like a winner and be somebody. Our company now employs more than 25,000 women who are winners and somebodies.

Freedom Our Birthright

Because I believe strongly in the free enterprise system and the ability of women, we at Home Interiors strive to place a value on each individual who is a part of this great organization. From the first day we met, December 5, 1957, we have had twin goals. These are like goalposts and everything we do must pass between those goalposts. Our goals are honoring God and serving others. Therefore, we consider progress as a new idea that fits between the goalposts of our twin goals.

We place a value on the *team*. There is no "I" in team and, because of this, we have other values. We put a value on work, the right use of money, and sharing our blessings. The object of living is work, experience, and happiness, and these values give that.

I heard an Israeli statesman say, "No nation or society, no culture, rises any higher than the standards of its women." So we have sought to place a high value on the standards—behavior, speech, service, dress—that bring out the greatest in each individual. Since all of our sales field personnel are women, we place a high value on the dignity and importance of women, family, and the home.

A long time ago Alexander Graham Bell, who built the greatest communication organization ever, said, "Great discoveries and improvements invariably involved the cooperation of many minds." I may be given the credit for having blazed the trail, but when I look at the subsequent developments, I feel the credit is due to others rather than to myself.

Value and Service

At Home Interiors we have given much thought to our purpose, and our purpose has been to give value and service. Value, service, and price—these are the three things people look for. We also place a value on integrity. Integrity is the first step toward true greatness and success. If we want to give real service, we must add something that cannot be bought or measured with money—sincerity and integrity.

We place a value on training before a salesperson goes out to sell. Therefore, we have all of our sales staff go through a two- or three-week "pre-case" training time; we are the only company in all of direct selling that does this. We are interested in each person who comes into Home Interiors and is issued a case of merchandise to show and sell. We want each displayer to find success and make money the Home Interiors way, to be able to find excitement and fulfillment in her life, and to still be home when the kids get home from school while growing as a person and a homemaker.

We invest time, effort, and money as she invests time, effort, and money, for we place a value on her self-confidence. We want her to be able to go out with confidence from the very first day she starts professionally selling for Home Interiors and Gifts.

All of this comes back to the value of the person, the value of the individual. Everyone is somebody! Each person on the home team and the field team is somebody! We thank God for what He has enabled us to do through His wisdom and His guidance, and we accept the honors and accolades for our twenty-seven years. But again, we must remind ourselves that they are seeds which have blossomed into fruit, which will turn into more seeds for the next generation.

TIPS FOR SUCCESS

1. Always make sure of your purpose before you go into a business venture—look for the best possible way to succeed.
2. Place a strong value on integrity—both personal and professional. This is possibly the strongest point I can make.
3. Always remember that everyone has a value, and it is up to you to fulfill your own personal values.
4. Set realistic goals, goals that are clearly defined. Goals that are too vague are seldom reached.
5. Add "royalty" to the routine. Find excitement in everyday work by adding a touch of royalty. Our slogan, "Think Mink," means the best—don't think rabbit or squirrel. Be good to yourself.
6. And remember, don't ever be afraid of tomorrow; God is already there.

"Donna Epp, emotionally immobilized by the death of her five-year-old daughter, created a business and in the process began to live again.**"**

Donna Epp
President, Creative Fabric Design, Ltd.
Deer Park, New York

I really went to school just to get what we used to call the "Mrs." degree. I wanted to find a husband, have children and a home, and be a housewife. For ten years, I was happily married, involved with my children and my hobbies, truly enjoying life. All of it fell apart when my daughter Lauren became ill. The diagnosis was cancer and from that moment on I spent every minute focused on her and her needs. When she died I felt as if I were dead, too.

Dealing with Grief

Eventually, my husband began to deal with his grief and encouraged me to try as well. I remember going with him to a St. Patrick's Day party in an attempt to join the world again. The next morning I couldn't move. I felt as if my whole body were in pain and I began sobbing. It was the first time I had actually come to terms with the fact that Lauren was dead.

In late April I was pregnant and nine months later I gave birth to a baby girl. Then I became pregnant again. After my fifth baby, my doctor asked me to come in to talk with him. He told me I could continue to have children or I could start raising the ones I already had. It was time, he said, for me to start becoming a whole person again. That was the very thing I had been afraid to hear. I thought I had failed as a mother because I had failed to keep Lauren alive.

What the doctor was really saying to me was that it was time to get on with my life and to make a decision on my own, for myself. This was so important because I had always been very happy letting others make decisions for me—my father when I was a child and later, my husband. When I looked back on the journal I had kept during Lauren's illness, I realized that I *had* made decisions. My mistake was thinking that I had failed because my love and energy and attention had failed to keep Lauren alive.

I came to terms with the fact that we all have failures in various stages of our lives in many different areas. Some of these failures are major and some are not. But even with the major failures you can stop and try to understand why you failed, what you could have changed, and what you really had no control over. I learned I was not responsible for the major crisis in my life but I was responsible for how it was affecting me, my future, and the people around me.

Beginning Again

So I began again and part of that beginning was to think about what I wanted to do and what I could do. I took business and design courses and even got a resale number even though I still couldn't figure out sales tax. The smartest thing I did was find a business partner who could. Diane Wulf had been my friend for thirteen years and she has the "money" and "marketing" mind.

The only "credentials" I had were a mother who never let me say, "I can't" and a father who started college at age thirty-nine and got his doctorate when he was fifty. Their achievements gave me hope that I could go a long way with very little visible assets except a determination to follow through and work hard. My father had been a high school dropout who achieved his goal of obtaining an education. Diane Wulf's background was similar; her parents encouraged her to attend the Tobe Coburn School for Fashion Careers where she was motivated by the women in design and fashion who served as trainers at the school. She decided early on that she wanted the fulfillment and financial success that comes from being your own boss.

Our business started as a small sewing business in our basement and is now a full scale factory workroom, Creative Fabric Design, Ltd. We came into the business in a roundabout way as a natural outgrowth of items we had sewn at home. At the outset, our limited experience making homemade drapery for our own homes was sufficient to allow us a decent profit sewing for others. By investing a minimal amount of money and working at home we were able to juggle our family responsibilities with our work. Eventually, we were confident enough to rent legitimate space and move our business out of the home.

We knew that there was a need for workrooms in the residential and contract interior design field where people in the trade could see our window and wall treatments. Today, the business has grown to a full-scale factory workroom and we employ a staff of ten full-time workers and many subcontractors as well.

We are somewhat maverick in our approach because we are not afraid to express and create designs that have not been tried before. We also found out that women like dealing with other women. We pay attention to detail and believe in keeping our word. What we say we do, we do. Our reputation began to grow when buyers realized that we stood behind our work and the installation of that work.

Preparing for Success

We not only establish long-range goals but have the ability to stick to the task at hand. In our business, preparation is very important and we have to constantly be aware of the designs that will be in for the next season. Whenever possible we try to combine the dream with the practical.

Because we don't have a strict "drapery" background, we were careful to spend extra time running the actual sewing and fabrication end of the workroom. Diane, who is willing to attack a technical problem and master it has chosen to be the workroom and employee supervisor. I am the salesperson, making initial phone contacts and visits necessary to develop a rapport with potential clients and current accounts.

Diane and I worked together to solve initial management problems, time scheduling problems, problems that all mothers have balancing work and home. Our husbands pitched in and helped in whatever way they could from babysitting to installing draperies.

All of a sudden we were relatively successful. When the International Society of Interior Designers asked us to donate our services to refurbish the Ronald McDonald House, where children and their families can stay while the child gets treatment at a nearby hospital, I felt as if my life had come full circle. I had spent so many hours there when Lauren was ill and it was a thrill for me to be able to donate our services in Lauren's name.

Today we are on the edge of becoming one of the largest comprehensive workrooms in the trade, and this will be another challenge—one I am ready for.

TIPS FOR SUCCESS

1. Develop a list of realistic goals.
2. Determine the time frame within which you will achieve those goals. Your deadlines should be as realistic as your goals.
3. Interview banks and do business with the bank that will meet your needs as your company grows.
4. Utilize any free space you have at home before taking on expense for overhead.
5. Research your business needs, including geographic area, market potential, income, and competitors.
6. Reconcile your financial needs. Be honest about assessing your personal financial needs and those of your business.
7. If you have children, make it a priority to obtain quality child care, even if you have to pay more than you'd like. It's worth it and will free you from worrying.
8. Be good to yourself and invest in clothes, your health, your overall appearance.
9. Increase your knowledge of business etiquette. Quality of service counts!
10. Avoid stereotyping images. Don't be afraid to be feminine, even if you are competing with men.

"Among the first women to graduate from the Harvard Business School, Barbara Franklin had to overcome traditional ideas of women in business to climb the corporate ladder and eventually start her own firm."

Barbara Hackman Franklin
Owner, Franklin Associates, Management Consultants Washington, D.C.

Have you ever experienced the "invisible woman" syndrome? It can happen in meetings or classrooms, when a woman brings up a notable point and the discussion goes on as if she hasn't spoken. Later on, a man may raise that identical point—sometimes even in the same words—and then people take notice. And you want to say, hey *I* said that! I remember sitting in a classroom at Harvard Business School, twenty years ago, feeling sometimes like the "invisible woman." At that time, there were only about thirty women out of 1,200 students studying under an all male faculty. Women in business, particularly women earning their MBA degrees, were rare.

Harvard Business School

Attending Harvard Business School was one of the pivotal points in my life. I could have just as well ended up in law school or earning a PhD in Education—both of which I was considering at the time. What happened was this: the dean of women at

Penn State University called me into her office and said she would like to nominate me for a scholarship to Harvard Business School, which had just opened its doors to women. I thought it over and agreed. I was admitted, offered a scholarship/loan arrangement, and entered Harvard Business School the next fall. I will be forever grateful to that dean of women—going to Harvard Business School is something I would not have thought of on my own.

In addition to having a first rate learning experience and earning an MBA, my experience at Harvard sensitized me to some of the difficulties women must overcome in a business environment, created and populated mainly by men. During my last year, another woman student and I did a research study to analyze the male students' attitudes toward their women classmates.

We learned that a majority of the women attending Harvard Business School were first-born children. We developed our "son-theory"—that fathers raised their oldest daughters as sons, giving them special attention and encouragement.

In my case, this was certainly true. I am the older of two daughters, and my father was by far the most influential person in my life. He was a role model, mentor, and friend. He had high standards for excellence, integrity, and hard work. He encouraged and supported anything I wanted to undertake—the only stipulation was that I do it well. While most of the environment in which I grew up was very "traditional," in terms of the "women-are-expected-to" attitudes, my father's support of my needs and desires to achieve made the difference.

Choosing the Corporate Route

After graduating from Harvard Business School, I headed into the corporate world with the goal of becoming the CEO of a major corporation. It never occurred to me then to start my own business. Women were not doing that then. I started out at Singer Company in New York at a salary that was about $3000 less than the average for my male counterparts. Nonetheless, it was good experience in both finance and marketing, and I joined the new corporate strategic planning group. At the time strategic planning was beginning to be recognized as a business discipline. It was my observation that women can often get ahead faster in new areas where there is both growth and fluidity.

My strategic planning experience led me to Citibank to be part of a newly created corporate planning department. As an assistant vice-president, I was one of only a few women officers. This was another good experience in a highly professional company on the verge of changing the financial services business worldwide. I was visible—and visibility to senior management within the corporate structure is vital for a woman who wants to move up. Perhaps this visibility was one reason that I was recruited to the White House to be the first person ever in any administration charged with recruiting and placing women in high-level positions in government. The man who recruited me was a Harvard Business School alumnus, as well, and I suppose he figured that since I was also a graduate, even if I was a woman, I couldn't be too bad.

Government Service

From 1971 to 1973, I, with the help of many other people, recruited and placed many women in high level positions in government—real "breakthrough" positions women had never held before. It was an enormous challenge, and I am proud of the record, which unfortunately, has been obfuscated by Watergate. But, in hindsight, one thing is clear: without the Presidential imprimatur which made the drive for equality acceptable, and without our successes in the early '70s the explosion of opportunity for women that happened in all sectors would not have happened so quickly.

In October of 1972, the Consumer Product Safety Act passed the Congress and was signed by the President. I was looking for women to fill two of the new commissioner slots when the president asked me to become a commissioner. I accepted, was confirmed by the Senate, was instrumental in creating the new commission, and served for nearly six years. I dealt with a wide variety of issues, regulatory and otherwise, regarding the safety and health of consumer products and gained expertise in the workings of government.

Back to the Private Sector

I decided to leave a year before my term was over, and knew I wanted to rejoin the business world. But overly strict provisions in the Consumer Product Safety Act, which has since been changed, prohibited my doing so for the next year. So when the dean of the Wharton School, the business school at the University of Pennsylvania, made me an offer to become a senior fellow, a special faculty appointment, I accepted. I lectured on government process and its impact on business. This allowed me time to reflect on my government experience (nearly eight years), and my earlier corporate work (about seven years). What to do next was a major decision. There were a couple threads in what I had done before—I had a history of creating new activities, having done that within each of the institutions with which I had been associated. I liked grappling with substantive problems. I liked making things happen, being independent, and having control over where I was headed. Without fully understanding it, I was moving into a more entrepreneurial phase.

At about this time, I received my first offer to join the board of directors of one of the largest companies in the country. Several more followed. I accepted this new role—it brought me back to the corporate world, at the very top. Then, I realized it would not make sense to re-enter the corporate beauracracy and try to work my way to the top. Large institutions still have a good deal of ingrained, unconscious prejudices.

The Evolution to Business Owner

Simultaneously, I was doing some intermittent consulting, advising consumer products companies about how to understand, deal with, and prevent health, safety, and environmental problems with the federal government. Then in 1984, as I recall it, I woke up one day and decided I was ready to turn this part-time activity into a business, which soon became Franklin Associates, management consultants.

The firm has grown since then, but is still small. I like it that way. I prefer working with those at the highest levels in the client company and with people I know. Our services are sophisticated, expensive, and have a distinctly personal touch. We are not lobbyists; we are, instead, interpreters and strategists.

With being in one's own business comes isolation and loneliness. You really are out there by yourself, especially if times are tough. Having a personal support system—spouse, family, and/or close friends—is very important to counteract this. But, on the other hand, being a business owner is creative, rewarding and fun. Being a boss brings independence and a real sense of self-worth. The effort is worth it!

A Personal Note

Clearly, my success has had its trade-offs in my personal life. I would like to have learned earlier to better balance the career and the personal life. I would have liked to have had a family, and I would like to have had some more fun recreational time. But, then, achieving anything requires choices and trade offs. What is important is to dream your own dreams and make them happen, and to keep doing that—always.

TIPS FOR SUCCESS

1. Want success and be willing to work hard for it.
2. Know what special talents and expertise you have. If you need more education or special training, get it.
3. Know who you are, your strengths, your weaknesses, your likes, your dislikes. Then, play to your likes and your strengths.
4. Have a plan. Devise a forty-year (or longer) career/personal life plan if you can. But be flexible enough to take advantage of unexpected opportunities and adjust to the bad luck in life.
5. Don't be afraid to think big—and take prudent risks to achieve your dreams.
6. Don't take yourself too seriously—be able to laugh at yourself.
7. Work at staying healthy. Success demands a lot of energy and stamina—physical, mental, and emotional.
8. Constantly work at being productive in the use of your time.
9. Think of yourself as a leader, and act like one.

"With hard work and confidence in herself, Claire Gargalli has become the highest ranking female in banking in the United States."

Claire Gargalli
President, Equibank of Pittsburgh
Pittsburgh, Pennsylvania

T he first step to achieving success is accepting the fact that nothing will ever replace hard work. There is no easy road. In addition to the hard work, you will need to recognize opportunity when it comes along and grab it. While you're waiting for opportunity spend the time increasing your technical and analytical skills.

A Lifelong Banking Career

I was named president of Equibank in November 1984 after joining the bank as senior executive vice-president in August of that same year. With that appointment, I became the highest ranking female officer of any U.S. bank. I came to Equibank from Fidelity Bank in Philadephia, where I was an executive vice-president, and also was the president of Fidelity's International Bank. Banking has been my career ever since my graduation from Middlebury College and my first job at Fidelity.

As president of Equibank, I am responsible for all of the bank's day-to-day operations and I am proud to say that under my direction, Equibank has consolidated its branch operations in fifty-five Pittsburgh area communities, and has expanded into the Philadelphia market with eleven newly purchased offices. As part of a three-member team that analyzed the bank's need to raise additional capital, I helped to execute a plan that raised $100 million during the past year.

Achieving Success

Have I worked hard? Yes. But working hard does not mean anything unless it's combined with working effectively or working smart. There is no secret formula but there are some important elements that must be present if one is to be successful. I believe they are as follows: Perform beyond expectations in the job you were hired to do. Next, figure out what else you can do (in areas related to your work) to help the company increase earnings, sales, or operating efficiency. Be an independent thinker. Come up with ideas yourself. Don't always be asking your boss, "What else can I do?" Once you decide what to do, estimate the probable benefits to the company and ask for approval to proceed. If you're not in a position to have all the information don't just do. There could be negative effects that you haven't considered.

On the Personal Level

On the personal level, you need to be adaptable—be able to adjust to your work situation, work demands, and other people—without sacrificing the core that is yourself. Remember, however, that before you can adapt to anyone or anything, you need to be comfortable with yourself and to feel secure in who you are and what you want.

It's also very important not to let little things get you down. Make sure if you're going to do battle you have your facts straight and you're absolutely sure that the issue is important. A rule of thumb I always use is to ask myself whether what is bothering me will have a long-term negative effect if it continues or is it just an annoyance. Dismiss the annoyances and get on with what's important.

Women are coming to terms very slowly with the concept of power. It is essential, as we achieve power as business owners, or within industry, that we understand how to handle it. We need to know the difference between power that's inherent in the position and personal power. If you can't separate yourself from the clout of a powerful position, you will lose all sense of reality as well as the ability to make intelligent decisions.

Gargilli

Finally, be good to yourself. Don't set goals that are too ri[...]
especially short-term goals. While you can't get ahead by v[...]
dering aimlessly, you need flexibility to take advantage of
opportunities. As you continue to achieve in the workplace, you
will find out what makes you feel satisfied. What makes you feel
productive or creative or proud? Be ready to be surprised and
enjoy the adventure.

TIPS FOR SUCCESS

1. Develop solid, top-notch technical knowledge.
2. Work effectively, not just hard. Respond beyond expectations.
3. Don't let small things get you down. Save the battles for major issues.
4. Be flexible, but know yourself and what's important to your personal and professional satisfaction.
5. Learn how to handle power.
6. Learn how to take risks.
7. Develop a sense of situation—read the environment and learn to react.
8. Set flexible goals.

Marilyn Koobation Hamilton, Don Helman, and Jim Okamoto, Owners of Motion Design, Inc.

"A devastating accident didn't stand in the way of Marilyn Koobation Hamilton's determination to be the best she could be.**"**

Marilyn Koobation Hamilton
Owner/Partner,
Motion Designs, Inc.;
Owner, R & M Dynamics, Inc.
Fresno, California

Why me? For twenty-nine years, I had carried on an active lifestyle—world traveler, beauty contest winner, skier, and high school teacher. Then one summer day in 1979, I found myself lying on the side of a mountain after a hang-gliding accident had paralyzed me from the waist down. I knew I was a very lucky young lady even to be alive. I also knew that living in a wheelchair was not the way I had planned to spend my life. I had always thrived on adventure. Would I now have to settle for being a spectator? Was my active life over? With plenty of time to think, I realized that nothing is absolute, that the only thing I could really plan on was change.

Aftermath of the Accident

The accident was definitely a big event in my life, but it was not the sum total of my life. I was determined to maintain just as active a lifestyle; I just had to learn to do things differently.

Fortunately, a generous dose of encouragement kept me moving forward after my accident . . . my family and friends helped me help myself. It took a lot of people and a lot of warmth, but they kept me going, kept me doing, and kept me inspired.

I'll never forget the time my friends and I took a ski trip to Mammoth Mountain, California. Off they went skiing while I sat, snowbound, visualizing the wonderful runs they were having in the fresh air surrounded by blue skies and snow-heavy pine trees. There was just one thing wrong with my skiing picture—I wasn't in it. Somehow I had to be out there with them.

The following winter I entered a program that taught me how to sit-ski in a Fiberglass sled using short poles. By the end of the season, I had won the National DisAbled Ski Championships in Slalom, Giant Slalom, and Downhill events at Winterpark, Colorado. I maintained the titles for three years, and was a member of the United States DisAbled ski team in Switzerland in1982, winning the silver medal in the luge competition.

An Inspiration

My chief inspiration at that time was my Uncle Bill, the most dynamic person I have ever known. In his teens Uncle Bill became a quadriplegic, but motivated himself to become a very successful businessman and lawyer in an era when disabilities were truly limiting. Through his encouragement and direction, I tackled new challenges, including becoming a produce broker selling fruit throughout the world for the family firm. I loved this new experience, but found myself yearning to be physically active again. I didn't realize that my craving to be mobile would provide the groundwork for a brand new company.

Necessity Breeds Invention

During the spring I began playing tennis. It was a frustrating experience. My conventional wheelchair (a real "dinosaur") just couldn't give me the mobility I needed to play the game. I needed a better wheelchair. Two friends of mine, Jim Okamoto and Don Helman, were starting to manufacture hang gliders, and I asked them if they could build a better wheelchair using hang-gliding technology.

We worked together to come up with the best design using the most durable, but lightweight, materials available. We sought the advice of medical experts and the disAbled community. Our efforts finally paid off. Our first"Quickie"wheelchair was ready for me to try.

The benefits to me were immediate—I became the Women's National Wheelchair Tennis Champion in 1982 and 1983. I took the chair everywhere I went including on the courts and on the slopes. Interest grew as more and more people saw that there could be a quality, lightweight, adjustable chair that even looked good. In addition to producing the Quickie wheelchair, Motion Designs was the first company to introduce a custom folding chair with modular frame construction. We moved from the sports market into the general market, then into the kids' market, and we're still growing strong.

Motion Designs literally began in Don's backyard garage. In five years we have become a multi-million dollar manufacturer with a 100,000 square feet plant in Fresno, California. Our chairs are sold worldwide. In 1984, we won California and Western United States Small Business of the Year awards, and have been honored at the White House by President Reagan.

Key to Success

The key to our business success has been recognizing and pooling our individual strengths and hiring winners in our areas of inexperience. We all committed to our dream to fill the void in a 30-year stagnant industry with our high performance Quickie chairs . . . it seems remarkable when we look back on our astounding success. All entrepreneurs should ask themselves: Is this product or service filling a need? If you answer yes, then follow your dream.

We learned to listen. In developing our first chair, we listened to medical experts, disAbled wheelchair users, my own needs and each other. We hired capable decision makers, many wheelchair users themselves. As we continue to grow, we've been able to respond swiftly to what we hear from Quickie owners, physical therapists and other medical professionals always keeping an eye on research and technology.

Don't be impatient. I remember that during therapy, my progress was always a series of little steps. Each one never seemed like much until I could look back at where I'd been. My motivation, my driving force, has always been to want things to be better, and I am thankful for each small step of progress. I've also taken steps backwards, but I know I've learned more from my mistakes and blunders than from my successes. Each mistake can help you make better decisions next time. Count your mistakes as progress—that way you won't feel so badly about them.

Believe in Yourself

Long before my accident I intended to be the best person I could be. My accident has opened doors and opportunities I never dreamed possible before. A banner year was 1985 when I was chosen California Businesswoman of the Year, one of America's Outstanding Young Women and was also invited to attend President Reagan's inaugural ceremonies as one of six citizens representing the public sector and business. I was chosen not because I'm in a wheelchair, but because Jim, Don, and I believed in an idea and worked to make it happen. Anyone can have an idea, but to succeed you must put commitment behind belief. Believe in yourself and your idea.

People often credit me with all sorts of extraordinary abilities, but that's really all nonsense. The only difference between me and most people is that I've been given a challenge people can see—I sit in a wheelchair. Because I've received so much help and encouragement, I try very hard to balance and share my life through involvement in a variety of organizations. I sit on the board of directors as executive treasurer of the Fresno Economic Development Corporation, and I am an honorary board member of the American Paralysis Association. I also serve on the President's Committee for the Employment of the Handicapped, am an honorary board member of the National CHALLENGE Committee on DisAbility, representative of the National Handicapped Sports and Recreation Association and the National Foundation for Wheelchair Tennis. As Motion Designs has grown, I have focused on advertising, marketing and promotion for our firm and have since begun my own advertising agency, R & M Dynamics, Inc.

The Difficulties

While I always try to look on the positive side, it would be unrealistic to leave you with the impression that I have had a smooth "glide" through my life, disAbility, or business success. I am one of the three percent of paraplegics who experience chronic pain and I have sought various treatments for relief and found that nothing has worked. I am constantly faced with physical function problems related to paraplegia aggravated by a tough athletic regimen.

I went through a difficult divorce from my husband of thirteen years who had been exceptionally supportive when I was first injured. Also, when my Uncle Bill died, I lost one of my most important mentors. Basically, I refuse to dwell on these adversities because they are all so debilitating they could make me feel truly disabled. They have the power to limit my mental and physical freedom. In fact, if I listened to some doctors I would never get out of bed. The road that I've traveled has not always been smooth; there have been many obstacles. But, I know that it is *my* road and how I travel it makes the difference. For every valley there is a moutain . . . and how I love those mountains!

TIPS FOR SUCCESS

1. Responsibility—You must desire to achieve the most with your life that you possibly can. When you face adversity, you have a responsibility not to quit. This desire builds character.

2. Challenge—Challenge yourself to go after your dreams. Don't compare yourself with anyone else or you will work to someone else's limits instead of your own. Focus your attention only on those things that you can control instead of wasting your energy on things that you cannot influence or change.

3. Commitment—To achieve your goals, you must commit yourself to do whatever it takes to get the job done. Prepare yourself both physically and mentally to visualize and push forward in that commitment—no matter what.

4. Perspective—Soar through life's problems. Always look for the good in every difficult experience. Have faith, even in the toughest times, that you can achieve your goal. Remember that most negative thinking contains gross distortions.

5. Giving and Receiving—Giving can be the easier of the two, especially for a giving person, but learning to receive is critical to achieve balance in your life. Drawing support from family and friends is vital in times of need; giving back in their times of need completes the circle.

6. Weathering the storm—Remember that on a calm day, *every* ship has a good captain.

> **"Mary Jo Jacobi, young and female, worked her way to the top—the White House and a major corporation—all before the age of 35."**

Mary Jo Jacobi
*Corporate Vice-President,
Government and International
Affairs,
Drexel Burnham Lambert, Inc.
New York, New York*

Who would have thought that a baker's daughter from rural Mississippi would someday be a special assistant to the President of the United States, and from there become a senior officer in a major Wall Street firm?

Politics and Business

Even as a child, I had a strong interest in politics and business, acquired from observing my parents' activities. I have been able to build a career that blends the best of both worlds, and have operated as a young woman in worlds dominated by older men.

In my parents' bakery in rural Mississippi, my sisters, brother, and I were taught the lessons of basic economics, mental toughness, and self-control (from exerting tremendous restraint in not consuming quantities of tempting sweets).

My father did all of the baking and my mother was the manager, bookkeeper, and chief sales representative. From my father I learned the value of hard work and dedication. I learned too the relationship between work and wealth—literally, how many doughnuts it took to make a dollar—and, beyond that, how many to make a dollar of profit.

From my mother, I learned the fine arts of salesmanship and persuasion and how to close the sale. There were times people would enter the bakery in search of the elusive birthday cake and leave with two dozen doughnuts instead. These lessons would serve me well in my career life, but my family also has served as a basic support network, encouraging my talents, cheering my successes, and soothing my failures.

Because our bakery was in the central business district of our little town, it was a hub of local political activity. Many discussions about politics took place and much gossip was exchanged over coffee and doughnuts in my parents' kitchen. These were the roots of my career: basic business sense, small town politics, and a supportive and loving family that never once questioned that a woman could do anything.

Like most parents of the Depression era, mine had the shared goal of providing better opportunities for their children than they had, which meant education. My parents didn't discourage us from an interest in the bakery business, but they believed that we should be able to choose our life's work for ourselves, with as many options open as possible.

Upon graduation from high school, I yielded to an interest in politics and enrolled in Catholic University in Washington, D.C., majoring in political science. That year, 1969, saw the height of the anti-Vietnam demonstrations in Washington, a year of student activism that culminated in Kent State. It was a year of disillusionment for me, and I transferred to Loyola University of the South in New Orleans and changed my major to the more practical, yet still male-dominated, curriculum of business administration.

Work and Education

Working my way through school was a necessity, and one of my first work-study jobs was student assistant in the office of the dean. Here I first experienced the value of mentors. Both the dean and assistant dean took an active interest in my career and my future, offering me advice and informal counseling and suggested reading lists. Both encouraged me to pursue a graduate degree and supported my applications for fellowships.

Still, despite their support and my own good grades, since women in college business programs were a relatively new phenomenon, I felt that to be on the safe side I should take shorthand and typing in case jobs were scarce after graduation.

In my final semester, I was awarded a teaching fellowship at George Washington University, graduated a semester ahead of my class, was selected for Who's Who Among Students in American Colleges and Universities and Beta Gamma Sigma National Honor Fraternity (the business school equivalent of Phi Beta Kappa).

In anticipation of beginning school in the fall, I departed for Washington to work as a secretary for Arthur Andersen & Co. It was there that I first learned the value of contacts. A friend of a friend told me about a position on the Republican staff of the Senate Commerce Committee. I couldn't believe it: an opportunity to be involved in politics after all!

What a heady experience it was working with senators, attending hearings and executive sessions, analyzing legislation, learning about power and politics first hand.

In Washington, I was learning, who you know is almost as valuable as what you know. Many times the resources of Capitol Hill came into play as assets in my evening graduate studies. Not only did I find myself right in the thick of a very exciting period (Watergate and the post-Watergate reforms, the Arab oil embargo), I also benefited from the work of the Senate Commerce Committee, which had a direct bearing on the issues I studied in my MBA program.

This perfect marriage of education and experience positioned me for the next career move. Where else should an MBA with Senate staff experience go but to lobby for business interests? That career move, however, was expedited by a crisis—my position was abolished due to an office reorganization. I suddenly found myself without a job and no plans for another.

My family and friends stood by me in those dark days of job searching. Their support gave me confidence that things would get better. And finally, after what seemed to be an interminable period of unemployment—actually only 90 days—I made the decision to take a sidestep immediately in order to move forward later. I learned flexibility.

My professional and personal contacts helped me secure a temporary position as a legislative aide with the El Paso Natural Gas Company, a six-month opportunity. This gave me employment (and a paycheck) and still afforded me the chance to look for something permanent.

Then one of those things occurred that one never believes will. During my unemployment days, I had a courtesy interview with the National Association of Manufacturers, where I was told that there were no openings but that my resume would be kept on file in case a vacancy arose. The NAM called, and I accepted a position as a staff lobbyist.

These were halcyon days for business lobbying, and we enjoyed victory after victory. I had the opportunity to handle the association's key lobbying effort, which gave me high exposure. Again, I found myself the only or one of few women in a largely male environment, serving on the steering committee for one of the largest and best organized business coalitions in the United States, meeting regularly with the leaders of America's corporations and working with members of Congress and their staff.

Visibility Path to the White House

This high level of visibility led to an exceptional offer to become the number two lobbyist for the very well-respected 3M Company. It is every association staffer's goal to move to a member company and I realized mine in just eighteen months.

The skills required of a good lobbyist are similar to those required of a good sales and marketing executive: the ability to communicate clearly and simply, and the ability to close the sale. At 3M, all of my communications skills were challenged. I had to relate not only to members of Congress and their staffs and other lobbyists, but directly with the top management of the company as well.

The company encouraged outside interests for its employees, and I became active in an organization to promote the professional development of women lobbyists, Women in Government Relations. In WGR, I was able to meet and share experiences with women in my field, and to hone leadership skills by serving on the organization's board of directors and in its committee structure.

Through networks like WGR, women have the ability to make friends and expand professional contacts, to learn from others similarly situated, and to identify role models. Some of the women I have met in organizations like WGR remain my closest friends today.

Another aspect of outside interests that 3M encouraged was political activity. I served as a volunteer for the Frank Wolf (R-Va.) for Congress and Reagan-Bush campaigns. After President Reagan was elected, this combination of personal and political activity led to my being recommended for a position at the Department of Commerce, working for the new secretary, Malcolm Baldrige.

Risk Taking

The original position for which I was hired—to coordinate the secretary's activities relative to the president's Cabinet councils, had not been my first choice. This was a new position, operating in a new system and it was unclear where this would lead me—up or down my career path. The safe and smart thing would have been to stay at 3M where I knew I was on the fast track. But I took the risk and accepted the job.

After serving only three months, I was moved in an acting capacity to head the department's Office of Business Liaison, and was subsequently named director. This was the position that had originally interested me. My decision to take the risk and accept another position in the hope that it might lead to something better had paid off.

As the demands of my position grew, personal time became a rare commodity. I had to make a conscious effort to maintain contact with my friends and family. Managing a staff of thirteen political appointees and career civil servants presented a tremendous challenge. There seemed to be no end to the number of meetings that could be scheduled in a day.

Again, long hours, hard work, dedication, and commitment, coupled with the support of a mentor (the Secretary of Commerce), would be rewarded. When the position as the President's liaison to business became available, Secretary Baldrige recommended me. It was very exciting to become, at thirty-two, the youngest person, only MBA, and first woman to serve as a president's principal link with the American business community.

Overcoming Prejudice

The issue of whether a young woman would be taken seriously by the captains of industry was raised, but surprisingly not by the men of the Reagan White House. It was raised by other women. The only way I could answer that question was to do the best professional job I knew how and work at it twenty-four hours a day.

I entered the position with the full support of many of the top business organizations, relationships that I had cultivated in my work on the Hill, at NAM, and at 3M, and that I had expanded in my responsibilities at the Commerce Department.

Serving on the President's staff is a once in a lifetime opportunity and an experience to cherish forever. But it is one of the most demanding positions in one of the most competitive climates in the world. It is, truly, the major leagues. At the White House, the job is always first and foremost. To be sure, the sacrifices yield rewards in the success of the President's programs, in the applause received for a speech delivered on his behalf, in the respect received from a responsive constituency, in the new universe of contacts explored in performing the tasks of the job.

This position called up my strengths and ferreted out my weaknesses more than any other, and my learning was done in the world's most visible classroom. They say that if you can last at the White House, in any administration, for a year, then you can last a lifetime anywhere else. I lasted nearly three years, and I learned through every moment of it.

The decision to leave the White House was a difficult one. After all, how do you top this? Because the White House is so special I don't think you even try but you do go on to the next challenge. This challenge presented itself when I was recruited through an executive search firm for the position of corporate vice president for Drexel Burnham Lambert, Inc., a highly diversified financial services firm in New York.

Return to the Private Sector

I view this move back into the private sector and the move to a new city as the next stage in my career development. In my years in Washington, I had done a wide array of things: worked on Capitol Hill, with a major trade association, for a large corporation, in an executive agency, and on the President's staff. I had observed business-government relations from every angle available in Washington. And now the move to corporate headquarters is a logical next step on my career ladder.

One of the most rewarding aspects of my positions has been working with the growing number of organizations representing women in business. Businesses owned by women are the fastest growing segment of the American business community, and more and more of the new professional, managerial, and technical positions are being filled by women.

We are the most dynamic force in the economic and political spectrums today, and it has been my privilege to meet and work with so many outstanding women.

A free enterprise system is a manifestation of an open society where opportunity exists for all. In a free society, enterprise is encouraged and achievement knows no bounds. Under this system, success and advancement are based on ability and hard work; under this system women have the most opportunity. But it isn't easy. It takes dedication and sacrifice.

Women in the Workplace

I don't believe that because I am a woman I should be given special advantages over others in the job market or anywhere else. I know that I have the capability to succeed on my own once I set my mind to it. We women want only the opportunity to expend our energies, compete in the marketplace, and pursue our aspirations on a level playing field. I believe that our free enterprise system provides precisely that.

Women have made tremendous strides in the American system. It is up to each individual to make her mark. In doing so, we increase opportunities for other women and for all Americans. The free enterprise system provides the climate in which each of us may realize our dreams and ambitions. It is up to us to provide the care and work to make them grow.

I truly believe that once the first woman accomplishes something, the opportunity tide raises all of our ships. In the last few years, we have seen so many firsts: the first woman in space, on the Supreme Court, as a vice-presidential candidate, as a presidential liaison. And each one of these has broadened the horizons and created new possibilities for other women. The more each one of us succeeds, the greater the success potential will be for all of us.

Building a career is a full-time task requiring constant attention and effort. It also requires the maintenance of a full and enriching personal life outside of a career, a difficult balancing act at best. We can learn from each other's experiences.

First and foremost is a support structure of family and close friends on whom you can rely in times of success and in times of stress. A well-rounded life is not easy to maintain while developing a career, but it cannot be postponed until you make it. You need outside interests to maintain your sanity.

A mentoring relationship with a key decision maker in your business can open doors and lend encouragement to your efforts. Exposure in your chosen field can build your credibility and vastly expand your horizons. Force yourself to take advantage of opportunities for public speaking, writing articles, moderating panels, and the like. In addition to providing visibility, it will enhance your self-esteem and hone your communication skills.

The wide array of professional organizations offers a great means of networking. They can be excellent sources of information on developments in your industry, job openings, and social contacts. The more people you know, the more your opportunities grow.

One thing of which I have been particularly proud in my career is the willingness to take risks, to leave a sure thing behind in pursuit of a new challenge, to sidestep in order to step up. I believe that the most successful people are those who are willing to do the things that frighten them the most.

Hard work, dedication, reliability, and commitment do pay off in most cases. If you do the job assigned to you in the best way possible, it is likely that the next promotion or position will take care of itself. The new opportunities will arise; talent is recognized.

Which leads to my final point: be open to change; listen for opportunity knocking. Even in what seems to be a terrible situation, there is usually a fantastic opportunity if you are tuned in to hear its knock.

I believe that I am proof that the system works. Coming from a small town, with a family wealthy with love but not necessarily material possessions, I have had the opportunity to break new ground, ground that once broken, cannot be resealed.

TIPS FOR SUCCESS

1. Take risks. Only then can you achieve your true potential.
2. Have a support staff of family and friends that can help you whenever you need guidance.
3. Have outside interests in order to remain fresh on your job.
4. Get into a mentoring relationship with someone who does what you aspire to do. Learn from that person and do what that person does.
5. Take advantage of opportunities to expose yourself in your field. When the opportunity to make yourself known in the field arises, take advantage of it.
6. Join a professional organization that gets you known. The more people you know, the better chance you have for advancement.
7. Work hard with yourself to do the best job you can.

"Penny L. Kerry had to overcome self-doubt about her ability to succeed in the male-dominated world of architecture.**"**

Penny L. Kerry
President, PNI, Inc.
San Francisco, California

I was born on March 1, 1942, in Great Falls, Montana. When I was very young, my family relocated to Pullman, Washington, where I grew up, went to high school, and married young. Without a clear sense of direction, I drifted along that path followed by so many women, attending book-keeping and secretarial school.

A Series of Jobs

To support my son and put my husband through college, I embarked on a series of administrative jobs. Whether you called it senior clerk, administrative assistant, or something else, I was a secretary. With the perspective obtained by serving for more than a decade behind a typewriter, I believe that the position of secretary is grossly underrated in terms of importance and pay. I also feel, however, that this job offers the best possible learning opportunities. In my years as a secretary, I learned everything I use to run my business today.

Starting as a junior clerk for the local telephone company, I learned about unions, budgets, corporate hierarchy, pettiness, sexual harassment,, and the value of friends in high places. After three years I advanced to Advertising Department Secretary for a small manufacturing concern where I learned about progressive management ideas, advertising, printing, corporate intrigue, and the risk of having friends in high places. After another three years I moved on to be sales secretary at IBM; here my exposure to *excellence* in product, service, personnel, and ethics formed my ideas of how to really run a successful company.

Better Opportunities

My husband and I decided to move to San Francisco hoping to find better opportunities there. It was there that I met my mentor, when he interviewed and hired me as the Architectural Department secretary for a nationwide construction firm in July 1970.

Less than a year later, my mentor decided to start his own private architectural practice and, at his invitation, I decided to join him. Initially the company was limited to the two of us, but we added staff as projects warranted. He was responsible for the architectural and sales end of the business and I was responsible for the administrative and interior design portions.

My initial duties were routine in any small business, from making the coffee to bookkeeping to secretarial work to client sales calls. In later years, secretarial work gave way to supervising clerical staff and becoming responsible for client contact, as well as the complexities of cash flow projections, business forecasting, and interpreting profit and loss statements. By necessity I was the liaison with our attorney, accountant, banker, and insurance and real estate brokers. No training was given, it simply had to be done and I was the only one there to do it.

Success Brings Changes

During this time, my husband and I grew apart. I was beginning to discover how challenging the business world was and that I could someday be more than a secretary. He had reached an early mid-life crisis and was soured on business success. We divorced very amicably with no alimony or child support to be provided, at my request. Although unplanned, I remarried within a year to someone who shared my energy and career aspirations.

In early 1977, my mentor developed cancer. I accepted the full responsibility for running the company, hiring additional staff as necessary to fill the voids. The staff performed admirably and we continued to grow and expand. In September of 1977 he died.

Although we thought adequate precautions had been taken, when the attorneys and accountants were finished I learned we had made serious omissions. The worst was the failure to execute a legal "buy-sell" agreement and to spell out a method of establishing a value for outstanding stock. While my mentor and I had agreed to a purchase price shortly before his death, the document was not technically legal. I was unable to reach an agreement with his widow for the purchase of her 60 percent of the company stock. After three months of legal battles and being told by my attorney that I didn't have a chance, I liquidated my stock and divested myself of company interests.

I don't ever want to go through that again. While I have experienced many traumas in my life, I believe this was among the most devastating. It was a relationship that can never be replaced and I owe much of what I have today to his seven years of mentoring.

Women in the Work Place

Women have brought a great deal to the work place, most notably, a widely established belief that women are much more humanitarian. While we still may not be totally accepted in the executive suite, we have effected changes in personnel policy. Flex time, pregnancy leaves for both parents, and corporate day care centers are all the result of working women. Our efforts have made the work environment more humane for everyone.

It has been speculated that as more women get into the business world, either they will change it or it will change them (i.e., make them more like men). Obviously, both things happen. I believe it is possible to strike a positive balance—for the benefit of women, and for the benefit of the business world and society.

My best woman manager said, "All the women who come to work for you wind up getting divorced." It sounds terrible, but these women had a great deal of potential but were very insecure. I try hard to give the women who work for me a solid steady dose of self-confidence. As they gain respect for themselves they are less likely to keep themselves in an unpleasant or unproductive personal relationship.

We are in an era when women are discovering their potential, and, therefore, their self-confidence, only after they have been married for several years. Their emotional and intellectual needs change as their careers mature, and they find that the common interests once shared with their spouses are no longer enjoyable. As new generations of women are raised with greater self-esteem, equal partnership matches will become more prevalent and divorces will be less common.

Our free enterprise system offers something you won't find in great abundance elsewhere: the opportunity to create. Whoever thought, in 1890, that the horse and buggy would be replaced? Whoever thought, in the 1920s, we'd ever entertain ourselves with anything but radio? Who would have guessed ten years ago that there was a consumer market for computers?

In each case, someone *created* an opportunity with imagination and hard work. Such inventiveness, and the freedom to pursue it, has powered our economy for two centuries. Ten years ago *I* never thought I'd be doing what I am now. But I do take pride in thinking that my company exists and provides career opportunities for many people because three of us believed in what we were creating.

Biting the Entrepreneurial Bullet

On March 9, 1978, I bit the entrepreneurial bullet and started PNI. Although I've been involved in the architectural field since 1970, the decision to start my own firm was not an easy one, nor one made without a great deal of apprehension. I knew by experience the problems of starting a business, and was not certain that I even wanted to stay in the very frustrating field of architecture.

Among the earliest professionals, architects have a great deal of responsibility and are notoriously underpaid. Creative and sensitive professional designers, they are also a very difficult group of people to manage. But as my mentor once said, "The one true happiness comes from solving a problem."

With two former co-workers to handle architecture and administration and me to sell their work, we decided to risk a year or two of our lives and our combined savings of $10,000. Committed to success and rapid expansion, the three of us moved into a very spacious 2,400-square-foot office in San Francisco in March 1978.

To say that the first year was horrible is a gross understatement. Self-doubts and unnamed phobias were ever present. Unknown to anyone, every morning on my commute into the office I played the tape of Helen Reddy's "I Am Woman" to give me the determination to face the day's challenges. I would sometimes sing along. Just singing phrases like "I know too much to go back and pretend" built up my self-confidence and helped me understand that other women were facing and conquering their challenges too. I have often thought I owe part of PNI's success to Helen Reddy.

It's Never Easy

Historic perspective has shown me that each year is easier than the last, although problems are ever present, ever changing, and ever frustrating. What really happens is that you gain self-confidence and know that you will be able to solve whatever problems are presented. It must be understood, however, that it is never easy to own your own business.

It is also lonely at the top because only you know how tenuous the entire company is; it is a secret you never can tell. At least once a week I vow to close it down and get out. Fortunately those thoughts are fleeting!

PNI survived the first turbulent years, and in the process established two wholly-owned subsidiary corporations: DKM Construction Company, a general contracting firm, and Interiors Purchasing, Inc., which supplies interior finishes and furnishings to PNI clients. Since 1980 we have been able to provide "turn-key" facilities to our clients: design the building, build the structure, and furnish it. Few firms offer this option nationally.

Because our professional reputation was growing, we received some national media attention. I grew bored with the status quo in mid-1983, so we decided to accept another challenge; marketing our company on a nationwide basis. This decision led to the opening of an office in Washington, D.C.

Although we took a substantial gamble, it has proven successful and has added prestige to our image with California clients.

The toughest part of entrepreneurship is getting a solid company foundation established. Once it's there, it is much easier to add additional "floors."

It didn't take long to discover that if you do the best job you know how, if you care about your customers, nearly to the exclusion of all else, and if you surround yourself with good employees, success can be achieved.

TIPS FOR SUCCESS

1. If you don't know where you're going, you'll wind up somewhere else. Plan your career path. Get professional help if necessary, but know where you are going and how long it should take to get there.

2. Don't get pigeonholed in a job. On your climb to the top, remember to diversify your experience. Ten years of experience is much more valuable than one year of experience ten times.

3. Life is too short to spend the majority of your working hours doing something you hate. Only stay at a job if you enjoy it.

4. You are capable of doing anything you want to do if you want if badly enough.

5. Superwoman is not a myth—it is a requirement for achieving women in the marketplace. We must be better, faster, and smarter. Fortunately, that's easy for us.

6. Do not sacrifice your femininity in order to fit in with the guys. Accept your sex with pride and let your compatriots and superiors do the same.

7. Join and participate in women's professional groups. They are absolutely essential to your success and sanity.

8. Your personal life is personal! Expect to have problems with your spouse or "significant other." Everyone does, so don't bore your co-workers with the details.

9. Understand that most men are either uncomfortable with or threatened by achieving women. Relate to their problems with our intrusion into the marketplace. You'd be the same, you know, if roles were reversed.

10. Never blame your sex for not achieving; that is a cop-out. Don't accept a roadblock; just detour, even if you have to backtrack a little.

"Dr. Lila Kroser's drive to become a doctor enabled her to triumph over the roadblocks of prejudice in the male-dominated world of medicine.**"**

Dr. Lila Stein Kroser
Physician specializing in gerontology and family practice Philadelphia, Pennsylvania

I knew from the time I was a child that I wanted to become a doctor. I wanted to care for people and become a part of their lives. Can you imagine wanting something so badly and then being told you can't have it because you're the wrong sex? No other reason, just you're a girl and girls do not become doctors.

Negative Attitudes

The first roadblock I had to overcome was negative thinking on the part of others—closely followed by my own self-doubt. What were my peers and society saying? Women cannot become doctors because women are not able to deal with the demands of the medical profession: long hours, heavy responsibilities, little social life. *Women*, they said, *could not make the commitment and the dedication medicine requires.*

Were they right? How could I find out? I began by making a list. On the negative side I wrote down all the reasons why I should not become a doctor. All those reasons offered by everyone else. On the positive side I listed reasons why I thought I'd make a good doctor. I found out that many of my "feminine" characteristics such as caring for others, listening, emphathiz-ing, were qualities that were very important to have as a physi-cian—whether man or woman. Was I ready to work long hours? Yes. Was I qualified mentally and physically to take on a lifelong commitment? *Yes*, I answered; *I was ready to make the commitment.* Was I mentally ready to become a doctor? *Yes.* Was I prepared with the knowledge I would need to achieve this? *No.* But I was prepared to make the commitment to get ready.

It was after midnight when I finished my negative/positive lists. I had put down everything I could think of and it was now clear to me that there was no *real* reason why I should not follow my dream and become a doctor.

An Important Step

That was a very important step for me and one that I took with the blessing of my parents. As an only child surrounded by the love of an extended family, I was given a strong religious up-bringing in an environment open to new ideas and new chal-lenges. The sanctity of the Jewish home and the need for mutual trust and faithfulness both in the home and the workplace were traditions of my heritage. Many of the decisions, life problems, and conflicts that I observed in my extended household, differ-ences in male and female attitudes, observances and respon-sibilities, influenced my decisions in adult life.

My parents were supportive, assertive, and loving. Especially for those days and times, they were most mindful that I be given equality of choice for study, profession, or career. My parents never graduated from college, but they never stopped learning. My father was always reading and studying and told me often, "Whatever you put in your head, no one can take away from you. So always aim for the top." When I was particularly dis-couraged about my chances of becoming a doctor and wondered if I should try nursing instead, my mother and father took turns saying, "Remember, the nurse only follows the doctor's orders. Be your own boss, be the *doctor!*"

Although the times were against me, my parents provided encouragement. I knew the home and family were important. I also knew that one's work was important.

Unwavering Ambition

All through high school my ambition did not waiver. College, however, was a revelation. I was the only girl in the pre-med courses. I was the oddball—and often the butt of jokes and pranks. Suddenly, thrown into the world of men, I encountered resistance from "my son, the doctor" types. Ironically, my nonaggressive feminine qualities forced friendship and respect instead of disdain and I became "one of the boys."

Everything I had been told was true. The hours were long; my courses were hard. There was never enough time to do those things everyone else seemed to be doing. There were times when I wondered if it was worth it. But through it all, I was excited and energized by the possibilities.

My next hurdle was medical school. Even though my grades were excellent, the medical school associated with my college bluntly told women applicants "Forget it." All the old reasons resurfaced, plus a few new ones. "Women do not bring credit to the profession." This is a familiar story to those of you who are trying to break into a nontraditional career field.

A Career in Medicine

I was lucky that Philadelphia, where I lived, was home to the only women's medical college in the country with classes made up entirely of females. The number of women enrolled nationally was about 5 percent of total enrollment, with a minimal support network that had very little power or economic influence. No one told us how to set up a practice or how to combine a career and marriage; by working together, we were able to share information and advice and provide moral support to one another.

Although the words *mentor* and *network* were not in anyone's vocabulary in those days, I can say that I did have a mentor in Catherine Sturgiss, my professor of preventive medicine at the Medical College of Pennsylvania. Catherine encouraged me to stick to my goal of becoming a doctor and to always keep before me a vision of succeeding. She was able to make me understand that no one, not parents or friends, could keep me from being a doctor. But they couldn't do it for me either. My parents and Catherine provided the support and encouragement I needed and I credit them with enabling me to finally arrive where I am today.

I also began to network, although that word was not in anyone's vocabulary either. I joined the American Medical Association and the American Medical Women's Association. I became an active member in my local AMWA branch which served as a true network for personal support and shared experiences. Next, because I had a talent for financial tasks, I rose from treasurer of my branch to president. I became chair of the National Finance Committee, Archives chair, and Scholarship and Loan chair—the last a position I hold today.

The First Step

Graduating from medical school was only the first step in a long journey. I married a fellow medical student and together we went to the bank and told them, "Here we are. We have no money. Our families do not have money. We have two medical degrees and a lot of wedding presents. Will you lend us money to buy a house?" They did and we did. We set up our separate practices and it suddenly hit me—*I was a doctor!* It was (and still is) a wonderful feeling.

The next hurdle I faced was when I was denied privileges at the hospital closest to my office. I was told, "You can't be a wife, mother, and doctor at the same time." By now I was used to finding roadblocks in the strangest places. I simply took a deep breath and obtained staff appointments at every other hospital around.

In the ensuing years, I was not only a doctor and a wife, I was also the mother of three children. Because our residence combines my office and our home, I have been able to schedule appointments with patients not only at a time convenient to them but also at times that allow me to take part in my children's school and athletic activities, as well as our family's religious life.

I have come to believe that most of the roadblocks to achievement are obstacles that others put in your path. Today, with all of women's gains and accomplishments, sexism exists. When parents bring their children to see me for the first time they often think I am the nurse and not the doctor. I must sweep away that obstacle time and again. Every successful woman, I am sure, has her own, similar—and similarly recurring—obstacles.

Work is the Key

As a physician, entrepreneur, wife, and mother of three, I, like all working women, continue to search for more hours in the day to do those things I love and those things I must do. I chose to stay in general practice because it is interesting and challenging and it touches the greatest number of people. I believe person-to-person ministering is what medicine is all about.

I also realized very early that I would need help to juggle the various components of my life—family, home, and work. My parents and my husband have provided this help. As women and as entrepreneurs we must become more adept at utilizing help where we can find it. It is not a disgrace to say that *we are not superwomen; we can not do it all.*

Today, as president of the American Medical Women's Association, I work on publicizing the successes of women physicians and promoting an understanding of world health and social problems. In my own practice I continue to identify ways in which I can increase the quality of health care for my community and be a better doctor. I have also opened my office to students to teach them how free enterprise can function in medical practice. From the beginning, I was determined to provide care to the economically deprived without charge or at reduced fees. I have been able to do this and it has given me much satisfaction. In my capacity as chair of the Student Scholarship Loan Committee of the American Medical Women's Association I have liberalized and expedited the procedure for students to secure loans for financing their medical education.

In 1984 and 1985, I was able to carry the message of quality medical care in a free society to the People's Republic of China and the Soviet Union. I am convinced that high quality medical care is best delivered by the private sector to free citizens given free choice of health care providers.

As a member of a generation whose opportunities go beyond our mothers' wildest dreams and whose struggle to achieve in our own right has no precedent, I encourage each of you to keep your dream in front of you. And when your dream comes true, help others achieve theirs.

TIPS FOR SUCCESS

1. Know your heritage, who and what you are.
2. Have faith in your ability to succeed and balance your personal needs with your professional requirements.
3. Seek a broad-based educational program that encourages educational curiosity in areas outside your field.
4. Seek a relationship with a role model or mentor who can provide guidance in your chosen field.
5. Join organizations that can provide personal support and a springboard to major professional and community involvement.
6. Develop your managerial and decision-making skills. You can do this whether you're a housewife or a career woman. These skills will serve you well in whatever profession you choose. Dare to decide and start now!
7. Be a positive advocate for yourself and your profession. Negativism kills enthusiasm, creativity, and achievement.

"A desire for less fattening, more nutritious fast food made Barbara Krouse the mother of Lean Cuisine.**"**

Barbara Krouse
Vice-President,
Product Development,
Stouffer Foods Corporation
Solon, Ohio

I guess my claim to fame is that I am known in some circles as the "Mother of Lean Cuisine." I have worked with Stouffer's since 1969 and I've been in my present job since January 1982. My career began with the company when I accepted a job as a research assistant. In two years I was promoted to assistant manager of research and development and then manager of the department the following year. My next step up the corporate ladder was director of product development and quality assurance. It is in this position that I have been able to let my creativity flow and feel as if I have a challenge every day.

New Product Development

As a working woman I knew a lot about challenge. One I could never seem to conquer was what to fix for dinner after a long day at work and nothing "fixable" in the refrigerator. How often I wished I could just push a button and the perfect meal would appear, ready to eat in minutes, tasty and nonfattening. That wish became the base on which I built the concept of Lean Cuisine—a single-entree dinner containing fewer than 300 calories. This line has grown rapidly in the four years since it was introduced and has created a revolution in the frozen dinner category.

Another product that was close to my heart was pizza. I didn't like the frozen pizza available because the crust was thin and nothing like the restaurant pizza I was used to. Others shared my quest for the perfect frozen pizza and we worked as a team to develop Stouffer's French bread pizza.

Fast foods are a part of every working mother's menu but I was also concerned that fast did not always mean nutritious. Through cooperation between Stouffer's and the department of nutrition at Case Western Reserve University's School of Medicine, I was able to convince the company to set up an ongoing program on nutrition research. In 1984, Stouffer's established the Stouffer Fund at the university for that purpose. The initial contribution was $250,000 and the research conducted there will be available to the general food industry. Through the fund, the university's school of medicine will be able to study the link between nutrition and health.

When I was young, I really never knew that I would be doing this kind of work and I feel it is important to counsel young men and women who may be considering the food industry as a career. There was no one to counsel me when I was starting out so I counseled myself. The first attitude I knew I had to develop was an attitude of self-confidence. Without self-confidence I would never have taken risks because I'd have been too afraid of failure. It's a vicious cycle. If you don't take risks you never succeed either. I also had to learn to be less emotional, let people be people, and not take everything personally. This is all a part of the maturing process.

No Concrete Career Game Plan

I never had a concrete career game plan. But there were two goals that were clear to me: (1) do a good job and (2) take advantage of every opportunity. I never said, "I am going to be a vice-president by the age of thirty-four," but I did want it made clear by my attitude that I was capable of handling increased levels of responsibility.

Why are confidence and maturity important? With these qualities you not only help yourself but you also are in a position to help others. If you are a manager this is very important. My work puts me in contact with people all over the world. It is key to the success of our products that we all work together as a team, that everyone be encouraged to contribute. My definition of free enterprise is the ability to run a company in a way that is beneficial to both the consumer and the employee. It means providing the best service to the consumer who has freedom of choice. Free enterprise goes hand in hand with competition which stimulates everyone to do the best that is possible. It makes for a better company and a better product. I know the free enterprise system provides challenges and rewards that stimulate growth and personal satisfaction.

In a society without competition and freedom people do not find work fun and without fun there is no creativity.

TIPS FOR SUCCESS

1. Do a good job.
2. Take advantage of opportunity.
3. Allow people to be people; don't react emotionally.
4. Don't be afraid to make mistakes.
5. Develop confidence in yourself and act as if you have it until you do.
6. Share your knowledge and counsel with young people who are trying to break into your field.

"A late bloomer, Patricia Lindh began her career at the age of forty-five, long after her peers had become established.**"**

Patricia Lindh
Vice-President
Wholesale Marketing,
Bank of America
San Francisco, California

L ife does indeed begin at forty, or even forty-five. I started my career at that age. Not that I hadn't been working for the last twenty years or so. It's just that I never got paid for it.

An Inauspicious Beginning

When I graduated from college, I discovered that my BA in English was useful only in direct proportion to my typing speed. Shorthand was more marketable than a degree. So, like most of my friends, I attended secretarial school—briefly. Shorthand is the only course I ever flunked.

Eventually I went to work for an employment agency—no skills required—hoping that the dream job would cross my desk one day. It never did, but I learned something that became extremely important as I began my career years later—public speaking. I was asked to speak about the job market to high school senior classes in Chicago and that speech led to many others. In the process I became reasonably comfortable on my feet.

After a couple of years working on a commission basis, I came to the conclusion that a predictable paycheck had some merit. I accepted a position as an adoption caseworker with Catholic Charities. I loved the job and absorbed everything I could about it, including another useful skill which would serve me well later on: I learned to précis masses of information and to quickly dictate a finished text.

Life Overseas

In late 1955, having attained the princely wage of $65 a week, I retired, married, and moved to Singapore, where we lived for the next seven years. We were among the first generation of Americans to move abroad after the war and it was an exciting time for all of us. Here I finally found the opportunity to put my college degree to work. It was rusty and so was I. I co-founded and for five years served as editor of a newspaper which is still going strong in southeast Asia.

After spending two years living in Karachi, Pakistan, and Kuwait (where I became a closet feminist) we returned to the United States and settled in Louisiana. There I kept a promise made in Singapore. Having seen ourselves as others see us while living abroad, I decided to give half of my volunteer time to politics. The other half went to the usual civic organizations, where inevitably I wound up doing the public relations, editing the newsletters, and handling the media. It was great training and worth a college degree in communications. It also proved very beneficial several years later.

Politics was a challenge. Ninety-eight percent of Louisiana voters were registered Democrats. I was a Republican, a transplanted Yankee, and a budding, if moderate, feminist. However, after the required envelope-stuffing internship, I moved up the ladder to precinct chairman, parish (county) chairman, state vice-chairman, and national committeewoman. Along the way I continued to hone my public relations skills, adding speechwriting to my bag of credentials. I also learned how to staff and run an office, my first foray into management.

White House Appointment

In May 1974, Anne Armstrong, counselor to President Nixon, invited me to the White House and asked me to be her liaison with women's organizations throughout the United States.

Coupled with this considerable honor was my first paycheck in nineteen years. My husband and children shared my feeling that it was the opportunity of a lifetime. I took two months for them to rearrange their lives and then they joined me in Washington.

Following Anne Armstrong's appointment as ambassador to the United Kingdom, President Ford named me his special assistant for women, the first such presidential appointment ever made. Then, at the conclusion of the United Nation's International Women's Year in 1975, the President appointed me deputy assistant secretary of state for educational and cultural affairs.

Certainly the scope and duration of these three positions compelled me to maintain a speedy and nearly vertical learning curve. Fortunately, the years of volunteerism had helped to keep the skills I had acquired along the way reasonably up-to-market. There is absolutely no doubt, however, that the Washington experience provided the weight to my resume.

I have been with the Bank of America for the last eight years. I'm continuing to learn, to be challenged, to work hard, and I enjoy it. Perhaps that is the lesson in all of this. Never stop learning, never turn down a challenge, always work hard and enjoy it.

TIPS FOR SUCCESS

1. Learn as much as you can and perfect what you learn.
2. Never quit learning—there is always something out there that you can get to know better.
3. Never think a job is more than you can do. Your potential is unlimited if you just put your mind to it.
4. If you are not working, volunteer your time to keep your skills perfected and honed to a sharp edge. The volunteer route is an important one where you can benefit others while benefiting yourself as well.
5. As you climb and achieve, reach down and bring someone else along. Keep the chain going.

"Amelia Lobsenz marketed a talent for writing into a successful public relations business becoming the first woman to serve as president of a worldwide public relations association.**"**

Amelia Lobsenz
Chairman,
Chief Executive Officer,
Lobsenz-Stevens, Inc.
New York, New York

I entered public relations at a time when the profession, particularly at the top, was dominated by men. Twenty-five years ago most women in public relations worked primarily on food or fashion accounts and concentrated on so-called women's interests.

First Job

My first job was at an agency where I worked on the Associated Bulb Growers of Holland account. These growers were the 8,000 flower growers whose bulbs were exported to the United States. Our task was to encourage American producers to purchase Holland bulbs.

I helped the account supervisor in every way imaginable: writing newspaper releases, arranging publicity in national magazines and broadcast appearances for spokesmen, and developing marketing strategies for wholesalers. This was new to me, but I studied to learn what had to be done. I asked questions, I read up on public relations, and I took things home to study at night. Soon we were able to get a major hardcover book on gardening published by a quality publisher.

I also wrote articles about our clients for national magazines. I remember one year I located a bulb hybridizer in the town of Lisse, Holland, and I wrote an article for *Coronet* magazine on the scientific research that goes into bulb growing. We had reprints of that article made for distribution in hundreds of stores that sold bulbs. It explained how much effort bulb growers put into their product.

Soon my knowledge of magazines and my increasing understanding of public relations led to promotion to director of the magazine department, which I held for the next five years. This was perfect for me since I knew many editors and writers, and could suggest articles on behalf of my clients that often ended up in national magazines.

Such articles are highly believable and they reach millions of people who read and re-read them. Along with that potential for coverage, we often had reprints made for mailing purposes to potential customers.

Years of Growth

These were growing years for me, and I extended myself. Nothing was too much work for me. I volunteered to help write client programs, to visit overseas and domestic clients, to help out on all of the agency's accounts. Soon I was working virtually across the board on almost every agency account.

I went to Europe frequently to see our international clients. This international travel was to prove very valuable to me years later when I handled international accounts on my own and became active in the International Public Relations Association (IPRA).

Eventually, through friends, I was introduced to the public relations officers at the Rockefeller Brothers Fund, and was asked to personally handle public relations on the Rockefeller Reports, which covered matters of importance to the United States government.

This was a challenge I gladly undertook. I explained it to my agency employers, who agreed to let me work half-time for them. Also, with my boss' permission, I began searching for a replacement for myself as it appeared I was ready to start my own firm.

On My Own

Within a few months I had helped train a replacement and was operating my own fledgling agency out of my Manhattan apartment. Soon I got more accounts, including a major pharmaceutical firm, Endo Laboratories. I remember how excited I was when I walked up the steps of Endo in Richmond Hills in Queens and thought to myself, "This company is my very own client!"

Earlier, in my magazine writing career, I had done a number of medical articles. This ability to translate medical terminology into lay lanaguage proved to be very helpful in serving Endo and in getting other medical accounts.

In a short time I moved my offices from my apartment to the Squibb Building at Fifth Avenue and Fifty-Seventh Street in New York City. I hired more people, and began to expand slowly but surely.

Now I had a payroll to meet, high rent, and many other expenses. I never borrowed money, and I kept up-to-date on all expenses, but it wasn't easy. I viewed the business as a growing plant that I kept nourishing and watering.

The first five years were very difficult, but suddenly, in the middle of the sixth year, I knew that I would always have a successful public relations firm. And I was right. Somehow I had crossed a threshold.

The Agency Today

Today, my agency is number fifteen in size among independent public relations firms. We have net fee billings of more than $4 million and sixty full-time employees. We have some of the largest companies in the world as public relations accounts, and they represent important brand name products and major associations. We have travel accounts such as Trinidad & Tobago and Copper Mountain, Colorado; association accounts such as the American Optometric Association and the American Academy of Family Physicians; the New York State Lottery; Ciba-Geigy; Bankers Life; Renault; and others.

Recently, I was elected to be the 1986 IPRA president, the first woman to be selected in the thirty years of the association's history. This is quite an honor since IPRA covers sixty-two countries and its members are the leading public relations professionals in each country. No woman had ever been nominated for the presidency—much less elected.

I truly believe my election is a tribute to my goal-oriented attitude and my early steps of making a success in public relations in what was then a man's world.

TIPS FOR SUCCESS

1. Dare to be different. I didn't follow the route of other women in public relations by sticking to feminine types of accounts. I carved out a niche for myself as a woman who could be effective in a man's world.

2. Find your own particular skills that you can take into the work force. My skills were writing magazine articles and a knowledge of the magazine field. These special abilities helped me get started and led directly to my rise in the field.

3. Don't ever stop learning. I went into public relations as a trained magazine writer, but then I had to learn public relations. I took reading material home every night and weekends until I mastered the craft.

4. Acquire specialized and technical knowledge whenever possible. Our world is getting to be increasingly specialized, and we all need to be apart from the crowd. My experience in doing medical articles was a factor in my being able to serve a pharmaceutical firm as a client.

5. Be willing to take a chance on yourself. I left a secure job to form my own business. I had no formal business training—just public relations and writing experience and common sense!

6. Be prepared to study, read, and learn about your chosen profession. I took books and articles home every night in the early years of my career. I am a great believer in research and am convinced that the answers are there if we apply ourselves.

Lobsenz

7. Aim high. I never refused an appointment or a challenge. I usually was able to succeed, but not always. However, my batting average was good enough that I felt encouraged to keep on trying.

8. Practice sponge techniques. This is the ability to learn from those around you.

9. Be objective. We all tend to think about ourselves. It's natural. But if you put yourself in the position of others you will be able to serve them and yourself better.

10. Be willing to be an apprentice. If you are entering a field that is new to you, don't hesitate to become an intern or an apprentice at first. Often, it is the only way to enter a new field, and if you select the right company, the training will be worth far more than a high salary.

> **"Ella Musolino's lack of skills and experience never kept her from seizing every opportunity that presented itself."**

Ella Musolino
President, Sports Etcetera
New York, New York

It may sound ludicrous today, but when I was in high school I thought the only reason a woman would go to college was to either get a husband or become a teacher. Neither of those choices appealed to me so I decided to skip college and go to work instead. But what was the work going to be? I had no idea, no real goals, no strong career preferences, but I knew I wanted to do something interesting and challenging.

A Different Application

When I read an ad placed by the Atomic Energy Commission (AEC) asking for applicants, I decided to apply. I realized that there was no point in writing a long letter highlighting why I should get the job—my letter would be one of hundreds. So I sent a telegram instead. "I am ready to begin work immediately, I am enthusiastic, a hard worker, and I can do the job."

The following week I received my answer—I was to report to the Atomic Energy Commission and begin work in the compliance division. For the next two years I worked as a reporter for the division that was concerned with radioactive accidents. During that time I did do what was required and did it well. I also developed rule #1: Tell the client (customer, employer) you *can* do whatever is required—and then *do it*.

Two years was long enough to realize that I did not want to work for the government. Why not? I felt I was stuck in a pigeonhole where there would be no reward for excellence.

Education on the Job

My next challenge was with a small company originally established in England and specializing in financial printing. On my first job interview I was asked a series of questions all about tasks I had never done before but, again, I reassured the interviewer that I could do the work. The company printed stocks, bonds, and currency for foreign countries, and my job, which combined sales and service, put me in contact with many chief executive officers. This was really the beginning of my "master's program" in business.

Because I was dealing with high achievers I was able to see what professionalism in action looks like. I was able to compare different management styles and understand how they differed and why they worked. It was also clear that none of these executive officers was working a nine-to-five day. Their workday began early and ended late. I began to learn too, how important it was for me to understand that everyone has his or her own style and in order to make the sale the seller must adapt to the potential buyer's personality. For one executive it was important for me to go into great detail about our firm's services; others would say, "Just give me the bottom line."

As I began to improve my own leadership abilities, opportunities to take on more responsibility increased. I always said yes and then followed through with performance. Eventually I established a reputation for delivering what I promised. Slowly all of my lessons took hold and became part of my buiness personality.

A Change in Direction

When my company decided to go back to England I moved up to another printing company. This turned out to be a critical career move because it gave me an opportunity to meet former tennis great Bill Talbert. Bill did three things that shaped my future: he introduced me to tennis, he introduced me to the people involved with tennis, and, most important, he recognized the fact that I had organizational skills. This did not mean that I had a talent for keeping my desk drawers clean, but rather that I possessed a talent for seeing a problem from all sides in order to find the solution that will benefit everyone.

Bill Talbert convinced me that even though I did not know anything about the sports events business I could be successful in that field. I pretended more confidence than I really felt, left my job in printing, and embarked on a career that would finally bring the challenge I was looking for into my life.

The challenge: the U.S. Open, then called the U.S. Nationals, was becoming the premier event in tennis, but there was a problem; the event was not popular enough to guarantee a gate that could pay the prize money—$100,000—a substantial sum in 1968. Tennis was not televised in those days so sponsorship of an event did not have the appeal or outreach it does today. It was my job to figure out how to get the prize money. The first thing I did was make a list of corporations that I thought would want to participate as sponsors of the open. Next, I created a benefits package. What would a corporation get for sponsoring the event? There was a wide range of things we could offer in exchange for sponsorship: tickets, free courtside advertising, signage, hospitality suites for corporate officers and guests. For one company, we did a fashion show on center court. It all boiled down to one thing—find the benefit for everyone.

Increasing Success

I worked with Bill Talbert for six years and then I had an opportunity to become involved with World Team Tennis as general manager of the New York Apples. It was while I was working for the Apples that I met with my business partner, Bill Goldstein.

Even though the Apples did well, World Team Tennis didn't. So when I was asked if I would run the Avon Championships I jumped at the chance. The Avons have since become the Virginia Slims Championships, and I'm very proud to say that Bill and I have helped make it the most important event in women's sports.

In 1980, our company, Sports Etcetera, began to branch out into promotions. We now handle promotional budgets in excess of one million dollars for Merrill Lynch and other clients. We operate in a dual capacity, completely involved in the selling and administration of an event from start to finish, from tickets to towels. Our other capacity is as the buyer, locating and soliciting the right potential events for corporate clients and then implementing a benefit package. The work is rewarding, challenging, and creative. I feel very grateful that all of my career "detours" have led me to the presidency of Sports Etcetera, with offices in Madison Square Garden, in the heart of New York City.

For those of you who may be thinking of becoming entrepreneurs I would like to encourage your decision. I know there are unlimited business opportunities out there for women today. Be prepared to serve as an intern for a period of time. This is your learning period when you can perfect the skills you'll need later on. Be a sponge for information. Ask questions, watch, and learn. Have a positive attitude—it attracts people, ideas, support. Have faith in yourself and act as if you have confidence even when you don't. In time you will.

TIPS FOR SUCCESS

1. Expand on the skills you have and adapt them to other areas.
2. Let those in authority know that you are willing to take on added responsibilities, but be able to deliver on any promises you make.
3. Keep in contact with those you meet in business. Keep them aware of what you are doing and be alert to their career moves.
4. If you are a housewife and are considering going back into the work force, perfect some of your old skills.
5. Take refresher courses in your field.
6. Don't make a mistake and turn down a good offer because you don't know everything there is to know about what the job entails. Have confidence that you will learn as you go. Learn to take the risk and stretch beyond what you think your capabilities are. Your capabilities will increase every time.

> **"Disbelief on the part of her associates that she was anything but a housewife spurred Ruth Ann Petree up the entrepreneurial ladder."**

Ruth Ann Petree
President, Petree Graphics
McLean, Virginia

P etree Graphics and Advertising is not the result of a carefully planned effort to launch a business. That thought would have paralyzed me seven years ago when I began this adventure. In fact, I used to read books about success and wonder, "How do these people know exactly what they want to do? How can I draw my own blueprint for success?" I have since learned that you can succeed without a blueprint, you can even succeed if your map resembles a crazy quilt as mine certainly does.

Dreams of an Art Career Discouraged

As a high school graduate in the late fifties I was uncertain about a career. I had always been drawn to art but I was discouraged by my parents from pursuing this interest because they did not think I could support myself in the field. Detour #1 was when I gave up my dream of being an artist and became a flight attendant at the age of eighteen. A short time later I married a career naval officer.

Although my husband's career kept us on the move constantly and I had four children to raise, I managed to revive my creative and artistic skills by attending classes and seminars, talking with others in related fields, reading lots of books, volunteering my services, and asking questions. For those of you who are at home bemoaning the fact that the world is passing you by, take heart and realize you can lay the groundwork for a successful business by doing your research now. You will always find interested supporters who need your skills and enthusiasm. You may not get paid for your contribution but you will learn a lot and later you will see how valuable that experience was.

Starting Small

After years of gathering information and creating lots of givea-way art for the PTA, church, and community groups, I set up a studio in our home. Actually, it was only the guest room but it was an important step for me. I decided that no matter how often or where we moved, I would reserve this studio space from now on. I designed a business card, and without realizing it, I was in business. As my skills improved, my confidence grew. Without ever being fully aware of it, I was constantly selling myself. My manner had become reserved yet confident, and I refused to think about failure.

I loved the work I was doing at the time, which was a variety of crafts and calligraphy, a skill learned through two years of daily rigorous study. Gradually, the crafts fell by the wayside and my reputation as a calligrapher grew. In 1975, I opened a commercial studio. My rent was $50 a month. My studio hours were the same as my children's school day, and I brought work home each night. I took no salary and was astonished when, at the end of the year, the figures showed I had grossed $10,000. We were then transferred overseas, and Petree Graphics closed down.

Self-Instruction

I was driven by the need to learn more, especially in the area of graphic design. While we were overseas I read extensively about this fascinating field. I taught myself the equivalent of approxi-mately three years of formal graphic design training. I practiced my newfound skills on some small jobs I was able to find in my Italian community. In fact, I learned to work in Italian before I ever had my first job in English.

In Business Again

In 1977 we returned to the states. My children were now in their teens and I knew that what I wanted was to have my own business again in commercial, not home, space. In December of 1978 I found a small place that I cleaned and painted and rented, again for only $50 a month. While getting myself established, I took a class at the local college. Part of the class assignment was to participate in a national contest sponsored by RKO Radio. I entered and was a finalist. This led to my first real account with a local radio station where I was asked to do an ad that would appear in *Time* magazine. I worked on that ad day and night for weeks. I was definitely outside of my comfort zone in terms of experience, confidence, and understanding of the value of my work. The experience was both exhilarating and terrible. Exhilarating because there is a terrific high in getting work published and appreciated, terrible because I was scared of the unknown.

Because I considered myself a graphic artist, I had never thought much about the business end of Petree Graphics. I thought that having a license as the sole proprietor covered everything. I was an ex-housewife, in my late thirties, entering the world of small business in a field dominated by men. I had no college degree and no idea of the pitfalls I could encounter. I guess ignorance is bliss; it was for me. But soon I began working twelve- to-fifteen-hour days. I took no salary, lost weight and lost sleep. I was becoming a true entrepreneur and didn't even know the meaning of the word.

Petree Graphics

Petree Graphics grew slowly but steadily through referrals. I took every job seriously even though many were very small. I was getting real experience in the real worlds of graphic design and business. It was instinctive of me to study everyone I came in contact with. I slowly developed a sense of what professionalism is all about. I made a lot of mistakes. In fact, I think I made every mistake that was possible. I withstood a lot of stress while trying to grasp both the creative and technical aspects of my work and the thread of business expertise that was running through my mind at the same time. After a year, I was hooked and dead serious about making my business work. I was dimly aware that sometimes I was not taken as seriously as I wanted to be. I think being a woman requires more work and a greater dedication to achieve the same goals that a man may have.

In the second year of Petree Graphics I was still taking no salary and working seven days a week. I was, however, making an impression on the communities in which I was working. Petree Graphics was only one person, but I was becoming known as a solid, reliable, professional firm. I gained a lot of experience and information about the business end of what I was doing. I developed strong friendships with other entrepreneurs who are good friends and advisors to this day. After the second year, I was ready to take more risks, and also to start taking a salary. This was a big step. After that, I took risks more often.

Proud and a Little Astonished

Today I am proud, and still a little astonished, to report that my firm will gross over $1 million this year and has seven full-time employees with some part-time help as well. We are a unique firm of dedicated professional women, and I am gratified to look at our client list which includes some of the top corporations in the area as well as some national accounts.

This corporation is in existence because of the opportunities afforded by the free enterprise system. I never met with resistance or obstacles that I felt I could not overcome personally. Being a woman did not significantly deter me. I never thought that I couldn't go after my objectives. I took the free enterprise system and my opportunity to function within it for granted. My success or failure would have been my own. This system has allowed me to follow a path that began unfolding years ago. There would be no story, no success here without the opportunity afforded me within the free enterprise system.

While a driving ambition to succeed is key for success, many other attributes are necessary for one to prosper in the business community. To build constant success there can be no compromise. I believe in providing consistent, superior service with a lot of human involvement and warmth. All clients should be treated the same; the referral system bears this out. A small job has the potential of leading to something big in the most unexpected way. My employees are aware that I expect the same high standards of quality and service for a black and white newsletter as I do for a complicated, expensive color piece.

An All Woman Business

So far, Petree Graphics is an all woman business. They are zestful, enthusiastic young women of whom I am very proud. They have imparted to this company a special charisma that cannot be duplicated. To continue our growth we work hard to keep informed on the latest trends in our field. We are selling creativity but we are also experts in the technical aspects of our work. The technology is changing every day, and being informed and up to date is an absolute necessity.

My generation was raised in a society that molded us into roles as full-time wives and mothers. There was no emphasis placed on a career other than marriage. Today there is a new and healthy attitude that challenges women to pursue careers they were formerly denied. Women are free to become whatever they aspire to. The free enterprise system offers them the vehicle for the realization of the challenges they choose. Another enormous benefit is that women can now experience financial independence. It was with great pride and satisfaction that I observed my marketing director, a single mother of two children, recently purchase her first home. Because of the free enterprise system and the belief I have had in myself I have experienced a growth and actualization of potential that would have seemed impossible. Without this system it is doubtful that women like me who started careers with nothing more than enthusiasm and determination could have ever enjoyed the freedom of self-reliance and independence that I have found. If I have been able to accomplish any success or good whatever, I hope by reading this story other women will be inspired to take the risk and accept the challenge to fulfill their dreams.

TIPS FOR SUCCESS

1. Believe in yourself and have courage.
2. Be well informed in your field.
3. Be flexible and willing to change goals.
4. Seek the advice of others.
5. Respect every person with whom you deal.
6. Consider yourself smart and believe in your decisions.
7. Do not consider failure as a possibility.
8. Study and learn in the areas where you are weak.
9. Be diplomatic, but be strong and consistent.
10. Believe that you absolutely can do *anything* that you set your mind to.
11. Be fair.

Petree

"Barbara Proctor, from the wrong side of the hill in Black Mountain, North Carolina, conquered the roadblock of prejudice to become a successful businesswoman.**"**

Barbara Gardner Proctor
President, Proctor & Gardner Advertising
Chicago, Illinois

I grew up in a shack in Black Mountain, just outside of Asheville, North Carolina. My mother, who was sixteen and unmarried at the time, knew that the only way she would ever be able to support us would be to improve her education. She left me with a woman in Asheville and she went to Washington, D.C., to enroll in secretarial school.

Eventually my grandmother "discovered" me and she took me in to live with her. My mother sent money for my support to my grandmother but basically it was my grandmother who raised me. My grandmother was wonderful, a very strong woman who worked as a cook at the local college and during the summer was a maid. She was the guiding force in my life and I learned about work from her. She taught me so much including acceptance about what you can and cannot change. She had a great deal of faith in me and would tell everyone that I was going to amount to something someday.

The Winning Combination: Intelligence and Hard Work

I knew I was smart, if not beautiful, and it would be intelligence and hard work that would take me where I wanted to go.

Because I was a good student I received acceptances from several schools and chose Talladega College in Alabama where I majored in education and minored in English. My finances were helped by a scholarship, support from my mother, who was now working at the Pentagon, and my own part-time job.

After college, through Sid McCoy, who worked for Vee-Jay records, I went to work for Vee-Jay writing album cover notes. I also became interested in jazz and met many of the great jazz artists like John Coltrane, Miles Davis, and Nancy Wilson. *Downbeat* magazine accepted an article of mine and later when they were looking for a full-time jazz writer, I joined the team—working for Vee Jay during the day and listening to jazz at night. Eventually I became Vee-Jay's International Director and well known as a jazz critic.

I married during this time and it lasted only two years. The positive thing about this marriage was it resulted in my son Morgan. Unfortunately, my ex-husband, Carl Proctor, a road manager for Sarah Vaughan, felt threatened by my stature in the jazz community. After we divorced I quit my job in order to remove the possibility of running into him on a regular basis and I began freelancing again. This was a very bad time for me. I had left a glamourous life style and exchanged it for the uncertainties of freelancing.

During this period, the liberal sixties, I was approached by a man who represented an advertising agency. This agency felt it important to hire a black for image purposes but his heart wasn't in it. He was not sure how others at the firm would feel about working with me. This was a very humiliating time for me but the end result was good—I was now intrigued with the advertising business.

Taking Control

I joined a firm and became the first black working for a general market agency in Chicago. This was a great learning adventure, to go from writing about jazz to products and labels. Another good piece of luck happened in the form of Gene Taylor who, more than any other single person in the advertising world, is responsible for what I have done today. He was definitely my mentor in advertising and when he was fired I quit too. This was when the germ of an idea about owning my own business began to form. Unless you're the boss you really don't make decisions.

It was too late for me to start all over again in a temporary position so I thought I better get something that I could control.

I tried to get a Small Business Administration loan for $100,000 to start my own business but I didn't have any collateral. When banks asked me what collateral I had I told them I was it. When they checked my references they found out that my reputation in the advertising business was a good one. I got a loan for $80,000 and I was in business. This was the first service loan guaranteed by the SBA to anyone—male, female, black, or white.

Positive Business Standards, Quality and Dignity

I knew from the beginning that I would have certain standards regarding who I would or wouldn't represent. I did not want any client with a product which would adversely affect the black community or that would portray blacks in a negative way. I would refuse to advertise a company that portrayed blacks in a negative or stereotypical manner. This is important to me because I remember back when I was poor and living in Black Mountain, how I looked up to Lena Horne. She stood for something—quality and dignity. Because of the positive influence she had on my life I would like to think that I might serve as a positive role model for some child growing up today. My firm must reflect good images, strong values—not negative messages.

I also felt it was important for my agency to take a stand regarding discrimination on the part of radio stations that had predominantly black audiences but did not pay their black salespeople the same amount of money as their white salespeople. I was determined that Proctor & Gardner would buy air time for commercials on black owned and oriented stations whenever possible. We would also refuse to buy time for commercials on any white owned stations that had unfair hiring and paying practices. Many of my friends in the advertising community were surprised that I would take what they thought was a losing stand. I told them it may not be a winning position but it is a moral one. It was a winning position as well. My clients agreed with the position I had taken and stayed with me. That year I was chosen Chicago Advertising Woman of the Year.

TIPS FOR SUCCESS

1. It is important to find a way to achieve balance, and to have someone, some system that enables you to concentrate on the professional part of your life without worrying about the rest of the details.
2. Know where you stand and what you think.
3. Don't be demanding of others if you do not have high standards for yourself first.

"Marsha Sands began with a small coffee shop, built a renowned Los Angeles restaurant, and intends to introduce Paris to the pleasures of good American food.**"**

Marsha Sands
Owner, Camelions Restaurant
Los Angeles, California

My parents were immigrants who combined a strong work ethic with an equally strong love of life. The most important thing they taught me is that love of life itself, joy in being alive, comes before anything else. You can work hard, they said, and you can have a good time doing it.

I entered the business world only fifteen years ago in order to make money. I was not looking for something just to occupy my time or a job that would let me express myself creatively. I needed the money and financial security. But what could I do? I was a housewife who did a great deal of entertaining, but could I transfer this talent I had for entertaining in my home and market it until I had a viable, successful business?

First Venture

My first venture was a small coffee shop in an office building. I wanted to be able to close the doors at an early hour so that I could have the time to spend with my family and this kind of restaurant provided the hours I needed. It did very well and I sold it after one year to buy a bigger and better coffee shop which I owned for three years and then sold to open a new restaurant in Newport Beach, California.

I owned that restaurant for three years, and then sold it after I saw an ad in the *Los Angeles Times* for an inn in Nantucket, Massachusetts, on the shore. This sounded great to me, so I flew to Nantucket. It didn't seem strange to me at the time that I was ready to open a business and live in a place that I had never been before. One look at the inn and Nantucket and I decided this was for me. I bought the inn and ran it for three years. It was basically a summer business—Nantucket winters are very cold—and I really wanted something that would run year-round. I sold the inn and moved to Los Angeles where I felt confident enough to tackle the restaurant market.

Camelions

Much of my confidence was based on the fact that while I was in Nantucket I had discovered a nineteen-year-old girl named Elka Gilmore who was an extremely talented chef. She agreed to come with me to Los Angeles and help me open my brand new restaurant, Camelions.

I knew that the menu offered at Camelions was going to be in the expensive range so it was necessary to pick a location in an affluent part of town. It was also important that I choose a location where the local residents would enjoy dining. I found a fantastic old home that I remodeled into the restaurant. It has all the charm I look for when I dine out so I knew that, at least, I was pleasing myself.

Through my other ventures I had learned how important it is to watch your finances and I negotiated a lease that was very favorable to me, one that would allow me to reap a substantial profit. I was able to get the financing from the bank because of my reputation with my other restaurants. I did not have a financial advisor but I have always made sure that I knew everything about the finances and how they would affect my bottom line.

A few months after I opened Camelions in Los Angeles, my husband fell ill and within a short time died. I thank God for my business, which really saved me emotionally. Now I was really on my own—emotionally and financially. I would have gone crazy if it weren't for the business keeping my mind constantly geared toward something other than my grief. At that time more than ever, it was essential to my well being and livelihood that Camelions was and continued to be a success.

Camelions as it is right now came from many years of experience with starting small and looking forward to bigger and better things. I believe that this is why it is such a success. I made sure to learn the business from top to bottom before I set out for the big piece of the pie.

That, to me, is the biggest obstacle in the restaurant business. It is very hard to treat it as a business and devote oneself to it like any other business, because of all of the distractions that come from having a restaurant—you are always entertaining, and it becomes hard to be businesslike.

Old-Fashioned Hard Work

The only way to get around that is through old-fashioned hard work. This is the first lesson when going into business. Your needs and desires must be realistic. Too often, people approach doing things for the wrong reasons. Business requires hard, dedicated, committed work that must be grounded in reality. Only then can someone hope to be successful.

I am successful because of a combination of many years' experience and hard work. Everything comes together at a given moment in my business and I go with my instincts. In the restaurant business, you *cannot* be afraid to take risks. I have gotten to the position I am in now by making my restaurant the single most important thing that I do. I watch over it, worry over it, nurture it—I treat my restaurant like I treated my children, and, in fact, I think that the restaurant requires more time. To be successful, you can never slack off. You can't say to yourself, "Well, I don't feel like it today."

Advice on Starting Out

With this in mind, how does one start? It is difficult for the single-person entrepreneur. There is no company or corporation to start at the bottom with and learn by working through the system. If you want to be an entrepreneur and be a success at it, you are going to have to be willing to face going out on your own. However, it is not as hard as it seems if you approach the situation in a sound, practical way.

First, research the kind of business you want to start. There are many resources to help you understand entrepreneuring. Speak to people who are already in the business. Listen and learn. Find out from those in the business how much time and money may be required. Then double it. Do a cost analysis based on your information and instincts. There will be inaccuracies— terrible and costly ones—but you will have a framework from which to work. Be brutal when you are analyzing the figures. They will differ from the stories you may hear about the joys of being an owner. The figures will also point out the pitfalls that lie ahead. Random discussion is good for background but no business should be based on conversation. Spend some time thinking about the downside of what you are planning to do. Many times recognizing the hazards in your proposed business is more helpful than imagining the great wealth you are going to receive when you become a success.

Start Small And Learn

Start small and learn every facet of your operation. Work in the business yourself and have the talent to be able to step into any position and be able to do it just as well, if not better, than the person you are replacing. Since the company will be a small one, you will be able to control your operation while learning. Have patience in yourself and in your company. Many problems need time and reflection. Some right themselves without doing any-thing; others need to be thought through and may require more time. Hasty, quick-fix decisions solve old problems by creating new ones. Get to know other people who are trying to do the same thing you are, and work within the system—that lets the system work for you.

That tired and overused word commitment, none other, con-veys what is true of any successful endeavor. Your responsibility extends to the whole and therefore to all its successes and fail-ures as your business grows. Surround yourself with the best people you can find. I look for the young and the gifted. They bring their own creative ideas which are so valuable. Businesses are not run by just one person but are the work of many.

Changing Women's Roles

I have come a long way. By this I mean that I was not brought up in an environment or society that taught women to look at a career as a necessity, or as a way of life one would always pursue. It was only the extraordinary women in the past who thought that way. My generation chose the profession of motherhood and wife. There was little opportunity for anything else. We are all aware of the role of women thirty years ago. Today the world has changed radically. Women need to ensure their own economic protection. It is important that women take the view that men have always held: one spends one's youth educating oneself to enter the workforce with tools adequate to lead a financially productive life.

I chose a field that I believe is a natural for women and indeed it is one where there are many who are successful. Right now, we are seeing young women chefs who are changing the erroneous thinking that only men can excel in the culinary arts. America today is in the forefront of good cooking, and many women are leading the way.

This is a wonderful field for women—and there is a natural progression within the restaurant business for a woman to become an owner. I am going to take that step a little further with my next project. I am looking toward opening a restaurant in Paris. I think Europeans have a misconception about American food, and I think that we have something to contribute to Europe. I will be doing this in order to make a contribution to Europe and to myself.

TIPS FOR SUCCESS

1. Know your finances and research costs before you begin. Be realistic and plan ahead.
2. Keep learning in your field.
3. Work hard. Nothing will ever replace hard work.
4. Never slack off. Commitment is the number one requirement for success.
5. Learn all aspects of your business from the most menial job to the highest.
6. Have patience with yourself.
7. Never go for the quick fix.

"Barbara Schlagetter faced the obstacles of going for a 'man's' job."

Barbara Schlagetter
General supervisor, production,
General Motors Moraine
Engine Plant
Dayton, Ohio

Whaen I graduated from high school there just wasn't any money for me to go on to college so I went directly to work. I made up my mind that in order to overcome what I felt was a definite roadblock to success—lack of education—I would just have to work harder and smarter.

My first job out of high school was desk clerk at the Holiday Inn, followed by night auditor, secretary/bookkeeper, and finally, innkeeper. In three years I moved from entry level to manager status and was responsible for 208 rooms and 116 employees.

The job of innkeeper is very similar to that of an owner of a business. I was responsible for the success of my Holiday Inn, the satisfaction of the customers, and the productivity of the employees. My confidence in my ability to manage people, money, and time grew and gradually I became less anxious about not having a college degree.

A Lifestyle Change

When my husband was transferred, I gave up my job at the Holiday Inn and moved with him and our two boys to North Carolina. Our marriage ended in divorce several years later and I was faced with deciding how to re-enter the job market. What would I do? I planned to go back to work as an innkeeper but General Motors offered me a challenging opportunity—the chance of a career in manufacturing. I knew nothing about manufacturing but I did know something about management, so I took a deep breath and accepted the job. I knew I was taking a risk but I also knew that the rewards in the form of greater promotional opportunities would be there if I did well.

My friends told me I was moving into a very unorthodox career for a woman as production supervisor of General Motors, Inland Division, in Vandalia, Ohio. My responsibilities included supervision of the injection molding lines for the production of foam seats. Although I knew next to nothing about manufacturing, I had confidence in my managerial abilities and in 1980 I was laid off at the Inland Division. Then I was interviewed and rehired at the General Motors' Moraine Engine Plant, one of four women overseeing production of the 6.2 liter diesel engine.

My work is exciting and challenging and I hope I have been able to encourage other women to think in terms of nontraditional career paths. These jobs are steppingstones to the top. Until recently, women in manufacturing organizations held supportive roles in supportive departments. As new opportunities arise, women are assuming positions traditionally held by men. We are doing the work and doing it well.

My next move was to statistical process control facilitator, which was followed by a one-year special salaried employee-in-training position in preparation for a promotion to general supervisor of production. My selection for this program demonstrates that upper management recognizes that women can contribute to the efficiency, profits, and spirit of an organization at every level. This awareness on the part of management is opening doors that were once closed to us.

Women in a Man's World

As a woman in a man's world I have learned that women and men alike sometimes react negatively to a woman who is intent on climbing that corporate management ladder. This is where the women's network of business organizations can help. They provide an arena within which women can deal with one another as professionals and respect, encourage, and affirm one another's goals.

Schlagetter

What helped me along the way? The opportunity to supplement my education and take management training courses, courses in labor relations, financial seminars, courses in personal dynamics, applied statistics, industrial psychology, facilitator skills, and leadership training classes. Step by step, I built on the positives I knew I had and found a way to overcome the negative—lack of education. General Motors provided the ladder and I grabbed the rungs with both hands. The courses helped immensely, but I realized that if I were going to continue to climb within the corporation I would have to go to college and get my degree. I did just that and will graduate with a degree in industrial management from Capital University in Dayton.

Ingredients for Success

It is important to me to be a good manager, to listen, to remain flexible, to inspire, and also to be able to work as a member of the team. Ingredients for success? They vary but I would pick one key ingredient: balance or self-control. A balanced manager or employer is fair, is able to make decisions, strives to cooperate and to understand. A successful person must understand herself first. What kind of job do you see yourself doing? What sacrifices are you willing to make to get and keep that job? What is personally satisfying to you? What contribution do you want to make to your world, to your family, to your friends? Success requires that you set short- and long-term goals, concentrate on your individual talents and capabilities, and keep stretching.

It is also important for you to understand the strengths and weaknesses of your management style. The iron fist style of management that says, "Do it my way or else" is not a style I feel comfortable with. Based on my experience, I know that most people want to feel motivated at work and have an opportunity to contribute to the final product. If your staff does not feel that their contribution is important your business or corporation will be in trouble very soon.

As manager you need to get input from everyone. As a production supervisor for General Motors Corporation I share my experience and knowledge with my associates, whether they are paid by the hour or salaried. Our team goal is to manufacture a quality product. For example, here at General Motors the people on the assembly line sometimes know more about what is going on than the person in the office in a particular area. If I make an effort to listen, I can put together the information I need to make good management decisions representing many views.

Working Together

We are all working together to build a competitive engine at a competitive price that meets customer satisfaction. For all of us on the team it is important that the efforts we expend result in a quality product and satisfied customers.

Has it all been easy? No. I am the divorced mother of two children and sometimes my mothering responsibilities conflict with my job requirements. How do I solve the conflict? By communicating honestly with my children and giving them a sense of what it is I do and why I do it.

When I was growing up, I was told that my most important goal would be to get married and have a family and I did just that. My family is very important to me but I began to realize that my work was important to me also. Many women like me who went off to work in the mid-1970s found that they liked the workplace much more than they liked being home. There was no stopping us after that. The important thing to remember is that no job is a man's job or a woman's job. It's a job and women are capable of doing whatever they commit themselves to. As women continue to achieve we will ensure that the path becomes smoother for other women.

TIPS FOR SUCCESS

1. Get a good education. This is the most important thing that you can do for yourself.
2. Self-evaluate your skills and values. If you have an idea that you can do something, build on that idea and do it.
3. Be visible in a visible position. Take on increased responsibility and make sure you follow through with performance. Work toward that visible position where your talents will be noticed.
4. If you do not get the promotion, market yourself. Actively campaign for a job if you think you are the right person for it.
5. Be a risk taker. Have a positive attitude toward yourself, and take risks to get things accomplished.
6. Learn how to use empathy. Empathy is the ability to share another person's feelings and accept another point of view. Most successful people have this.
7. Identify a role model and listen and learn. You might find one at work or in one of the many excellent women's business organizations. Meet with other business women and exchange ideas, advice, and support.
8. Do not let little failures discourage you. Progress will come if you believe in yourself.
9. Have an open mind toward change.

> **"A** widow with no job experience, Marge Schott has made a name for herself in the male-dominated world of professional sports.**"**

Marge Schott
President, Owner,
Cincinnati Reds
Cincinnati, Ohio

Years ago I was a happy housewife doing all the homebody things that wives did in the 1960s. My tranquil homemaker life was disrupted overnight by the sudden and untimely death at the age of forty-two of my husband, Charlie. Overnight I became a widow with enormous business responsibilities to be resolved. Charlie left me with an auto agency, pig iron plants, a brick and block plant, an unfinished shopping center, and a multitude of other companies. But he never told me how to run them and I guess I never thought it was going to be necessary for me to know how.

An Unwanted Boss

In those days, no one had heard of the word Ms. or could spell it for that matter. It was understood that I would hire someone to take over and run the companies and I would remain very quietly in the background. The last thing the employees and management at my newly inherited companies wanted was me for a boss. If I had inherited my father's company it would have been a different story. I had worked for his Cincinnati Veneer company for a number of years and at least the staff there recognized that I knew the business.

The only thing I could remember from my father's business that made sense for me now was that one should stick by the company's people no matter what. This was a message I intended to follow with the companies that Charlie had left to me. Unfortunately, the company executives had other things in mind.

They all flew in to talk to me on the day of the funeral about the business and my plans. Most of them were giving me the "What do you think you're doing, lady?" look when I told them I planned to run the companies. I tried reasoning and working with them, but finally when neither worked I had to bite the bullet and fire those who would not or could not work for a woman.

Next, I appointed myself president and chairman of the board of all the companies—that way no one could fire me. I reassured all the employees that their jobs were secure and if they would just bear with me for a little while together we would all benefit.

Staying in the Automobile Business

The company that frightened me the most was the automobile business. The auto industry was very important to the Schott family and I wanted to keep Charlie's Buick agency. General Motors had never had a woman dealer in a major metropolitan area, and I was worried that they were going to take away something that had been a family tradition. I was right—they didn't want a woman running a General Motors agency, but after an almost three-year battle, General Motors signed me as a Buick dealer and, eventually, we became the number one agency in the Tri-State area.

As you might expect, with no public relations or advertising background, my television ads for the dealership were anything but run of the mill. I knew one thing; I did not want to go on television myself so I recruited my sister's kids and my St. Bernard dog, Schottzie, to help in the commercials. Sometimes I wondered if people thought we were selling dog food instead of cars. I was not used to dealing with the public, and my friends would say, "Oh Margie, you can't go on television kicking tires."

Common Sense Prevails

I did a lot of bluffing in those days, but soon came to the realization that good old common sense does prevail. I never looked at my involvement in the male-dominated business world as a woman out to prove a point, but rather as a challenge and a task I had to accomplish. I am the first to admit that I certainly did not know all I needed to when I began—but I learned fast. What I didn't know already, or couldn't find out from someone who did, I figured out and did it my own way in my own style. I believe this attitude also prevailed when I became the new owner and general partner of the Cincinnati Reds baseball team.

Baseball is a tradition in Cincinnati, and there was concern that a new owner might take the team away from the Tri-State area. I was feeling more confident, the businesses were doing well, so I began to look for a way to express my gratitude to the city. The people of Cincinnati had responded to my dealership, the ads; even my dog Schottzie had become a local celebrity. The logical way to say thank you was to make sure that the Reds stayed in Cincinnati.

Saving the Cincinnati Reds

I kept waiting for some of the businessmen in the community to step forward and ensure that Cincinnati would always have the Reds. But no one appeared, so I stepped up to the plate and did it myself by becoming the new owner and partner of the Cincinnati Reds baseball team. It became my Christmas present to the city. I love our fans and sit out in the stands, talk to, and sign autographs for all who come down to visit.

I am quite sure that the direct and honest approach that worked for me in business brings people into the park. The fans keep returning to Riverfront Stadium because we've got good players, a great team, and a family atmosphere. The children come to see Schottzie, who goes to every game, and get her autograph. Once you get down to common sense and the people principle, it really is almost impossible to fail. Before I bought the team, the fans were extremely turned off because the "Big Red Machine" had been broken up and no one was listening to their concerns. Knowing that someone now cares is a big thing for the fans. I strongly believe that without their support you have nothing and I try to make sure that they are getting their money's worth. At the last game of the 1985 season, I announced that there would not be any increase in ticket prices for the next year. So many poorly run companies pass on the costs to the consumers. I don't want this to happen.

Treat People With Respect

The same holds true in the automobile industry as well as other companies. Treat the fan or the customer or the client with respect and provide a quality product. I am a very strong believer in Buy American—sometimes I feel I coined the phrase. I think if anyone loves this country, he should be willing to support it by purchasing products produced at home. I have bumper stickers at my car agencies that read, "Buy American. Thanks, Marge Schott."

For an entrepreneur, whether a man or a woman, every day is a new challenge. With a greater sensitivity and responsiveness to employees and customers the free enterprise system will continue to grow and prosper.

TIPS FOR SUCCESS

1. Pay attention to details. I had to go to the first owners meeting, and some of those guys are heavy hitters. But by paying attention, it really helped me understand just what was going on.

2. Don't come in as a woman's libber—come in as a woman. It's still a man's world out there, and that suits me just fine, thank you. Women make mistakes in going into a business all gung-ho and saying "I am a woman, so treat me better." Men respect you if you come in low-key—not "Here I am, treat me better."

3. Appreciate what a man has to do. When my husband was alive, I was the typical housewife. But after he passed away, everyone was coming to me for decisions. There was no one on my left side or right side. I quickly began to appreciate what a strain it was for men to have all the responsibility.

4. Respect goes both ways. I want the man to respect me as a woman first, and as a business person second, and that should be the attitude that you take toward anyone, regardless of sex. If you want someone to respect you, you have to respect that person first.

> **"M**uriel Siebert was the first woman to buy a seat on the New York Stock Exchange making the male-to-female ratio 1365:1.**"**

Muriel Siebert
President, Muriel Siebert and Company
New York, New York

I was born in Cleveland, Ohio, and I moved to New York in December, 1954, literally never having been away from home before. I applied to the United Nations for a job first, but I didn't get it. That was probably a blessing, because by now I would probably be chief messenger girl with a bad case of fallen arches.

A Smart Choice

When I applied to Merrill Lynch they asked me if I had a college degree. I told them no and they told me that there was no position available. On my next interview at Bache & Company they asked me the same question and this time I said yes. I got the job. Bache & Company offered a choice; a back-office job in accounting for $75 a week or placement in training and research for $65 a week. I made what was the right career decision for the time, and took the lower paying job. You could get by on $65 a week then. Today, I pay more to garage my car than I paid for apartments for years.

I rose through the ranks, became a research analyst, and got some orders from institutions based on reports that I had written. This changed my income and my career drastically. I began to sell only those stocks that I had personally researched. I was a partner with three different firms, and then in 1967 I made the New York Stock Exchange co-ed.

Breaking Ground at
The New York Stock Exchange

A friend of mine suggested that I buy a seat on the NYSE. None of the 1366 seats on the exchange had ever been held by a woman, but there was no reason not to have a woman. I had to get a letter from a bank that guaranteed me the right to have a loan if I was accepted onto the floor.

Once they said the Stock Exchange couldn't admit women because the language on the floor was too rough. They also said it was no place for women because there were no ladies' rooms on the main floor. Those arguments sound antique, but they were made only twenty years ago. But, on December 28, my bid of $445,000 for a seat on the exchange was accepted, and I became the first woman to join the group.

I was the only woman for nine years. I was outnumbered 1365 to one, and those are pretty good odds. This was, I guess, my biggest roadblock. There just weren't many women downtown and there were some places a woman just couldn't get in. Now those rules have been changed because people have demanded that they be changed. But when I was starting the situation for a woman was very bleak.

When I started my firm on September 28, 1967, I started it as an individual member. Then we began to do research for institutions, buying and selling analyses. I felt there was something more we could be doing and changed the course of our business. On May 1, 1975, we went to a discount service and gave up research. That was the first day that members could cut commissions. In the past, the stock exchanges had set the rates and those were the commissions for most rates. Then, the SEC passed a law that commissions could be negotiable, which meant that you could bargain with your broker on any size order. That broke the old fixed rate. I knew that a change this drastic would open doors of opportunity for someone and I decided to take the plunge and open the door. We became a discount broker, which means that the only thing we really offered was the execution of orders; no research, no advice, and that meant changing my firm totally.

A Gutsy Move

This was a very gutsy move, because nobody loved us. It was something brand new. It was the first time in the history of the New York Stock Exchange that commissions were negotiable, and I was there the first day.

I left my business in 1977 to become the superintendent of banks for New York State. I put my company into a blind trust and it was run by other people, because when you can get a chance to become a regulator of something that is that important and that vital, you don't say to the governor, "Come back two years from next Tuesday."

I was appointed by Governor Carey to regulate all of the banks in the state of New York. The banking department in New York regulates about $500 billion, which is more than all of the other states put together. New York's biggest banks are bigger than any state agency because we've got the foreign banks, a lot of money center banks, savings banks, and New York is the center of financing. It was an important job, and I'm glad I had the chance to do it.

How to Succeed

I think that not everyone can take the stock market. It is an exciting job, and you never get bored, but you have to be tough. There are pressures. There are times you can't do anything right. The market is the market, and you have to learn to roll with the punches, you have to learn how to think, you have to learn how to read the newspaper and see different things in it, and not everyone can take that pressure. Some people like a more sedate job. However, I don't think anything pays any better than the exchange. It's probably the best paid business there is—at least the best paid one that is legal.

In order to succeed in this field, you have to be willing to put in a great deal of time. You have to study in advance, you have to analyze, you have to see what your risks will be, what your profit ratio will be. You have to be willing to take a chance. Sometimes you take chances, sometimes you don't. It depends on the market. It depends on what is going on.

I think we are a good firm because we can see things that often no one else can. We sent something out to our clients a year ago on the Federal Reserve, and we literally caught the upswing. Hard work is a part of it, luck is always a part, and taking a risk is always a part.

The meaning of success is not measured by money. Wall Street happens to be a place where if you are a success, you make money; but other fields have different rewards. People generally do well at what they like. Of course, you have to meet things halfway. When you get knocked down, just get up and start all over again. But set your goals high and don't let anybody tell you no.

TIPS FOR SUCCESS

1. Find a field you like because you will spend a lot of time at it.
2. Find a particular job you like because of the same reason.
3. Find people you like within the job. If you do those three things, then it isn't work—it's a challenge, it's a game.
4. Learn to be able to make mistakes and accept them. But you aren't entitled to make the same mistake twice—only once. Anyone can make a mistake once, but not twice.

"A professional setback gave Ellen Sills-Levy the impetus to become a successful entrepreneur.**"**

Ellen Sills-Levy
President, Custom Studies/ Financial Services, Simmons Market Research Bureau New York, New York

Sometimes I think of my love of business as a past life. I really have no recall when it started, because it was always there. I think it was a desire to make my own money so that I would be independent. Again, I don't know where that came from as I was born into an upper-middle-class home and was not deprived.

Early Emphases and Influences

My mother worked until three days before I was born and laid claim to being one of the few women of her generation with a business degree from the City College of New York.

Her mother supported her children by building a business in Poland while her husband went off to seek his fortune in America. Maybe it's not past life, maybe it's genes.

On my father's side, the emphasis was education and culture and he struggled to become an architect and an engineer. I suspect I'm a combination of both, but the scale tips a bit on my mother's side for drive and ambition.

It's hard to say who influenced me. It was everyone and no one. I absorbed impressions like a sponge and at the same created my own fantasies.

I must confess, however, that certain superficial stimuli made their mark. My mother had a group of women friends who were successful in business and, as a child, I loved their clothes and their stories of far-off places.

But the winner as the weaver of exotic tales, was my father's brother—Uncle Moe. Uncle Moe is a corporate attorney, an entrepreneur, and a venture capitalist. When I was young, I didn't know what a venture capitalist was, but I was fascinated by his stories of far-off places and beautiful presents.

Maybe business represented to me clothes, travel, but most of all a presence. I equated that presence with success. Now I recognize it as a confidence and a generosity of spirit.

School was always important to me and, like many other entrepreneurial people, we're all driven with a desire to learn and a desire to know. I was timid as a child and sat quietly observing. I looked, I studied, I learned, and I imitated.

But, some guardian angel always gave me the right role models. Parents; my godmother, Alice; friends; bosses; my former husband and friend, Dick—each in their own way, gave me sustenance when I needed it and criticism, both positive and negative.

Today's Women

Today's women are especially blessed because we have built an incredibly solid network. Much of my success I owe to the special guidance of very good women friends who pushed, coaxed, helped, and nurtured. Special thanks go to my friend, Susie Fisher, who taught me so much about making it while retaining solid values.

More than a person, I think what influenced my life was a negative trait—tenacity. The positive trait was humor. Whenever anyone told me I couldn't do something, I found it unacceptable. At sixteen, I got a summer job in a brokerage house and came home after one week and announced that I would major in economics. From my father's reaction, one would think I was going to take up a career as a white slaver. I majored in economics, with my mother's approval. It wasn't until years later that I discovered that my father did not want me in the business world because he was afraid I would be hurt. His own experience was based on the treatment of women in his field—architecture. Every now and then, younger women should stop and realize what it was like for women who were pioneers in different fields. Maybe these pioneers are the ones who influenced all of us the most.

But, life was not all sunshine and roses. There were hurdles, there was pain, there was frustration and disappointment. I think all of it happened in one year.

Setback as Impetus

It was the year that was. I was on a fast track, I was a hotshot, and nothing was going to stop me. Unfortunately, my bosses at BBDO had their own point of view. They passed me over as research director in favor of a man. To this very day, I do not know if my sex was the reason, but at the time, I felt very discriminated against. At the same time my professional life crumbled, my personal life fell apart. My marriage of nearly ten years ended with pain.

Pain, disappointment, lack of confidence are catalysts to reshape the core. I got stronger.

To run away, I took an overseas job with BBDO—in Germany. If BBDO had an office at the North Pole, I would have welcomed it. I did not speak one word of German. I knew nothing but the most negative things about Germany, and much to my surprise, it was a wonderful adventure. I learned a new language and built a new company overseas—Life Savers Bubble Yum (you can laugh at the name, but it made a lot of money). That was the turning point. I learned to be stronger and went through a personality change. I can't tell you why but I became more dynamic and finally acquired the thing I admired most in others, presence. If we are playing true confessions, I also learned a lesson in humility. Again it was the tenacity that got me through.

My personal life and my business life did not help or hurt each other. Each contributed to my development and I do not regret any experience personally or professionally. Incidentally, my ex-husband and I have maintained a friendship and we treat each other with respect and dignity.

Requirements for Success

As president of Simmons Custom Studies/Financial Services, I find myself in the position of interviewing job applicants and mentoring college students. I always share my enthusiasm for marketing research. Technical skills are not enough. To be really successful in research today you have to have marketing judgment and business acumen.

It's hard to pinpoint what contributed to my success. It's a combination of technical and people skills. To be a good problem solver, you need analytic skills, people skills, a broad perspective, and gut reaction. Marketing is a must. Public relations is a plus, and general business training is a must. In my field, a love affair with high tech makes the difference.

Working within the system is easy because I plot my own maverick course. You can work outside of the system, but not at the expense of other people. Your way may be different, but don't establish that difference by stepping over people.

I think I've gotten to where I am now because I'm exceptional at what I do. I work hard. I don't take professional shortcuts with clients, employees, or the community. I'm always willing to learn and never stop reaching for a better way of doing something and I reject any kind of smugness. The success comes in a balance of life, you have to play hard and work hard. You have to make a commitment to people as well as things. And, if I may be trite, you have to stop and smell the flowers.

TIPS FOR SUCCESS

1. Success demands good health and respect for your body. Treat yourself with proper food and good exercise.

2. Look your best. People respond to people who look good. That doesn't mean you have to be a beauty queen or even young. It means you take pride in yourself and present the most attractive picture you can offer.

3. Real magnetism is enthusiasm.

4. Be courteous to everyone. Never burn your bridges.

5. Define your goals, hold on to them, and work toward them. You only have one go-around, so make the most of it. Take chances, be firm of purpose, and be flexible.

6. Whatever happens, humor will get you through very tight situations. Laugh a little at the world and a little at yourself.

7. Make your commitment to people as well as things both personally and professionally.

8. Be open to change, challenge, and be ready to turn on a dime.

9. But, most of all, dare to dream.

Ellen Terry
President, Ellen Terry Realtors
Dallas, Texas

T en years ago I was a carefree Dallas housewife who thought she had the world on a string. My balloon was filled with affluence, security, family, leisure, a $200,000 house, a Mercedes, dance lessons for my daughter, soccer practice for my son, Junior League functions, shopping at Neiman-Marcus, charity bazaars, tennis with my friends. I was living the American dream, insulated by my protective bubble of the right groups and the right people. I felt immune to disaster.

The Balloon Burst

Then suddenly, and without warning, my balloon burst. Every bit of it floated away and beyond my grasp. I was hosting a Junior League meeting in my home when I got my first inkling that everything was not right in my warm, secure world. The doorbell rang and I answered it, poised to welcome another Junior League member to my home. It was not a league member but a middle-aged man who wanted the keys to my car in the driveway. The payments had not been made for months and he was repossessing the car on behalf of a collection agency. This was the first in a series of events that included complete and utter financial devastation, divorce, and a seven-month separation from my children while they lived with their grandparents because I couldn't support them.

I had no idea that the fairy tale life we had been living was a life we could not afford to live. I was a housewife who never questioned anything my husband did—certainly not finances. After he left, I learned about finances fast. I had never balanced a checkbook, never had to balance the savings account statement, never investigated our securities holdings. I had trusted completely. I had always expected to be taken care of, and now I was faced with the reality that I was now the sole support, not only of myself, but also of my two children. I was facing this situation with no visible resources or opportunities. Because Texas is a community property state, I discovered that I was well over $100,000 in debt.

If any of this sounds familiar, then you can probably understand how I felt on that devastating day in 1976. I would have to go to work but what in the world was I going to do?

Ostrich or Fighter?

My material assets were gone, but I did have a legacy from my childhood, a feeling of self-worth given to me by my parents. I was taught to be a fighter and not a quitter and I knew it was important that I get rid of feelings of self-pity before I became helpless emotionally. In a way, my feeling of self-worth had been on hold throughout my marriage; now I had to revive the strong self that used to be me. Since opportunity was not knocking at my door, I had to go out and look for it when what I really wanted to do was dig a hole in the sand and bury my head like an ostrich. What I had to realize then is that the choice was mine. Ostrich or fighter.

One of the first things I had to do was to learn to set goals. I think the reason many people don't achieve success is they don't practice regular goal setting. During my marriage, I never felt the need to set goals for my life. Now I know that goals are absolutely essential to accomplish anything worthwhile—not just in a business or a career but in your personal life as well. I now set goals for everything—every single solitary aspect of my life. And I strongly recommend that anyone who wants to live a complete and fulfilled life should prioritize their life and activities by establishing long- and short-term goals—and re-evaluating them regularly. That way you can get what you want out of life instead of having to want from life.

Terry

The process of goal setting and of achieving larger goals by accomplishing smaller goals one at a time was especially helpful as I faced the monumental task of starting over from the very bottom.

Facing Reality

First, reality had to be faced. I was well over $100,000 in debt, with positively no way to pay the money back. In order to pay the Internal Revenue Service, everything had to be sold: my house, all the furnishings, my jewelry and clothing—everything. All of my possessions—all my worldly security—were gone. I had no car, since it had been repossessed. I needed a job, and didn't even have a way to get to work. For six months, due to the loving generosity of some very special friends and relatives, I was lent cars to drive while looking for employment and embarking on a new career.

But what type of career could I possibly pursue? I had been a housewife and mother for ten years. I knew I didn't want to go back to teaching, and I didn't have any secretarial skills. I started out in the travel business, but the income wasn't enough to survive on. My brother suggested I go into residential real estate, but I knew I couldn't wait to collect commissions because I didn't even have enough money to pay my rent.

A Career in Real Estate

After much coaxing, however, I agreed to interview with a national real estate firm that had just opened a new office in Dallas. After my first interview with this firm, I knew deep down that residential real estate was the career I wanted. I became convinced that if I were willing to work endless hours the opportunities would be limitless. It took three more interviews to convince this company to pay me a small draw against future commissions. But I did go into the real estate business, and discovered for myself the creative, exciting career I wanted: a career that did not set a ceiling on my income; a career within the free enterprise system that offered a woman tremendous opportunities for personal and professional achievement and success. It was one of the most significant decisions I've ever made in my life.

The day after I passed my real estate exam, I wrote my first successful sales contract. And within the first 45 days of my new career, I had sold two houses and earned $12,000—more money than I would have made in a full year as a teacher or secretary. I will always be grateful to the company that took a risk and hired me, thus enabling me to realize my initial goal, which was to bring my two children back home to live with me and reunite as a family again.

By the end of my first full year as a residential real estate sales associate with the firm of Coldwell Banker, I was honored as its top Texas producer and the number two salesperson within the company on a nationwide basis. I had also discovered my talent for selling expensive houses, and carved out a permanent niche in a highly competitive field. I started moving toward other goals which, to many, might have seemed improbable at the time. But improbable odds have always been just the challenge I need to encourage myself that if I am going to succeed, it will be up to me to do it.

An Entrepreneurial Partnership

After two and a half years with Coldwell Banker, I formed a residential real estate firm with two partners specializing in quality homes in prestigious areas throughout Dallas.

In March 1981, I launched my own company, Ellen Terry Realtors. By the time it was a year old, we had firmly established ourselves as the fastest growing and most highly visible firm of its kind in the Dallas marketplace. Today, the company, which I solely own and head as president, employs more than forty sales associates who are among the top earners in their field, and has often been referred to as the Cadillac of residential real estate brokerage firms in the Dallas metroplex.

During the 1984-1985 fiscal year, Ellen Terry Realtors sold and closed more than $153 million in residential real estate, which brought the four-year total sales volume to more than $400 million. In addition to its phenomenal growth in the first four years, the company has established itself as a leader in the marketing of Dallas' finest properties by selling fifty-seven estates each valued at between $1 million and $3.5 million.

This basically is the story of how one can start from zero and truly achieve within the free enterprise system. I was at the bottom of the minus-minus-minus column, and I did not know where I was or where I was going, much less how I was going to get there.

Ten years ago, when my world seemed to be crumbling around me, I had the ability to get where I am today. But I could not see those resources at the time because I was so overwhelmed by what I was not that I was not focusing on what I could be. I am convinced that everyone has the qualities and inner resources that can guide them on their personal road to success. Attitude is the key. Studies show that success is 15 percent aptitude and 85 percent attitude. When I launched my career in real estate, I did so with absolutely no education in business or finance whatsoever, and no previous experience in my chosen field. But I viewed this situation not as an obstacle but as a challenge—an opportunity for personal growth and development. My hope for all who are starting out in a challenging situation is that my story will encourage you to reach deep down and recognize your own inner ability, your God-given potential to become all you can be.

Just have faith in yourself and a supreme being, be willing to step out and take risks, and be willing to fail, knowing that every time you fail, if you've learned from it, you are really failing forward.

There is a Price You Have to be Willing to Pay

It takes a lot of emotional energy and stamina, making choices, giving up certain things to reach higher goals; it can also cause turmoil if you don't pace yourself. Balancing the emotional, physical, spiritual, personal, and professional areas of your life is very important in order not to become entrenched in compulsive, addictive behavior.

I firmly believe that there are no restrictions on what you can do unless you create these restrictions within your own mind. I challenge you, I encourage you, I support you as a woman in the free enterprise system. Success is yours for the asking. But whatever your chosen field or endeavor, be committed to excellence.

Basically, the formula is both very difficult and quite simple. You have to *think* success. You have to look for possibilities. You have to view problems as challenges that can be turned into opportunities. Every loss in life can be turned into a gain.

TIPS FOR SUCCESS

1. If you think you can, or if you think you can't, you're right.
    You can get through anything, no matter how depressing or
    frightening. Look at each situation not as a problem but as
    a situation or challenge that can be turned into an
    opportunity.
2. Risk taking. My risk taking was handed to me. But without
    the challenge that adversity brings, many of us would never
    realize our full potential. Risk taking can be turned into a
    formula: insurmountable problems = challenges =
    opportunities. Just have faith in yourself and a supreme
    being, be willing to step out and take risks, and be willing
    to fail, knowing that every time you fail, if you've learned
    from it, you are really failing forward. If you find a path with
    no obstacles, it probably doesn't lead anywhere.
3. Self-image. Start acting confident now. A confident person
    talks, walks, and moves differently from someone suffering
    from a lack of self-esteem. If you walk and talk with gentle
    confidence, the people in your world will react accordingly.
    We can shape our own self-images. We can create our own
    successes.
4. Attitude. We are thinking, feeling human beings and we
    hurt when bad things happen. But we do have much more
    control over our destiny than most of us think. We can
    stretch to our maximum potential, and we can achieve
    whatever in life we want to if we focus on the possibilities
    and what can be done through belief and faith in ourselves
    and our own abilities and the people around us.
5. Goal setting. Anyone who wants to live a complete and
    fulfilling life should prioritize his or her activities by
    establishing long- and short-term goals—and re-evaluate
    these goals on a regular basis. Goal setting gives you
    direction. Without goals you are like a ship without a
    rudder, bounced around by good winds and bad, never
    knowing where you're going to wind up.

Terry

> **"**Barbara Vance left a lucrative career in real estate to embark upon an entrepreneurial venture as president of a speakers' bureau.**"**

Barbara Schmidt Vance
President,
National Artist Bureau
Washington, D.C.

As a former schoolteacher and real estate agent, and now owner of my own speakers' bureau, I credit my success as a multi-career woman to a home-taught appreciation of the work ethic and education. My lawyer father and school-teacher mother paved the way for me. These values are now being passed on to my daughter, Amani.

I like to bring a sense of drama, creativity, and excitement to my work situation. This, coupled with placing a premium on well-reasoned independent thought and action, has allowed me to confront life and business with a clear headed sense of adventure.

Reaching Out

I married at 24. My former husband was a fellow student at a small college in Cheyney, Pennsylvania. His intelligence, sensitivity, and drive eventually propelled him into the front rank of television broadcast journalists. When he was offered a plum broadcasting job in Washington, D.C., we decided to leave Philadelphia where I had been teaching. After the birth of our daughter, I thought it important to be a full-time mother during her early years.

My sense of adventure and wonderment were fulfilled in raising my daughter while my husband grappled with the realities of positioning himself in a fiercely competitive market. Our love for each other was never stronger so when I decided to venture into a new career he was very supportive. The real estate industry in Washington, D.C., was fascinating to me and in 1973 I became a real estate agent for the Begg Company. The opportunity to sell properties that I personally liked to strangers who needed advice and counsel in this area was an appealing challenge. I loved the challenge and in one year sold one million dollars of real estate.

Beginning a Speakers' Bureau

In the early 1980s my marriage had become another chapter in my life and now as a single working mother it was time to chart new seas. I felt ready to unleash my full creative energies on a brand new entrepreneurial endeavor. The idea of owning and running a speakers' bureau seemed natural. Agentry came easily to me and I enjoyed bringing together all the elements of a successful deal. My enthusiasm was high but I knew it would have to tempered with education. Marketing, establishing contacts with salable clients and interested employers, promotion, and drawing up individual contracts were areas that were going to require extensive research on my part.

It is to their credit that when I discussed my idea with two old friends, Ed Bradley of *Sixty Minutes* and Willard Scott of the *Today Show,* they unhesitatingly agreed to become my first two clients. Their confidence spurred me on as I made my daily trips to the Library of Congress to find out all I could about the establishment and operation of a successful speakers' bureau. In addition to researching the basics I began to make a list of the people I thought would be popular, informative, and entertaining on the speakers' circuit. Soon, I had over 500 names catalogued in file boxes.

I announced the formation of my new enterprise as the birth of a new baby. My promotional letter came complete with the picture of a friendly, avuncular stork. Soon after my first mailing, the phone began to ring—my business was off to a great new start.

In addition to representing outstanding speakers I counsel organizations and businesses enabling them to choose the right speaker for their event. In conjunction with this counsel I advise on media outlets and publicity for the event.

I wanted a challenge and I found one. In this business the unexpected becomes the norm. You have to be able to remain calm and come through with a solution for your client. You can't afford to get upset over every minor detail—you just have to solve the problem.

As part of my job, I have to communicate to whomever is in the market for a speaker that people in the public eye are not necessarily in the public domain. They get a fee for speaking and I get a fee for my work. With that fee comes a guarantee—this takes the risk out of events. If you have ever had the experience of having your keynote speakers fail to show at an event you're responsible for, you can appreciate the guarantee we provide.

Part of my success is that I tapped into a market that wasn't being properly approached. I began with local and therefore less expensive speakers. I work very personally with the employers and the budget, finding the right speaker at the right price. In many cases, this means I have to work a little harder but it also means I have referrals coming in at a steady rate.

I also realized that although my product was no longer houses, I was still dealing with a buyer and a seller and the goal was to find a creative way to bring about a mutually satisfactory transaction between the buyer, the employer, and the client.

To succeed in this or in any other business, you have to be able to take risks, you have to be able to assert yourself, and you have to be able to work long hours without the rewards until the very end. Am I saying that you must be a workaholic in order to succeed? I guess I am. Another key ingredient: you have to be confidently humble about what you are doing.

The bottom line is you have to be ready at that starting gate all the time. A lot of effort is required, but believe me, the rewards are there.

TIPS FOR SUCCESS

1. Plan your goals, but be realistic.
2. Follow up everything you do—clients, employers, everything.
3. Investigate the marketplace where you plan on doing your business. Knowing the who, what, where, and why sort of things are essential.
4. Make sure you have the basic equipment and materials.
5. Be firm but polite and patient. The buyer should always be encouraged to ask questions and eventually find a path of trust. Without this trust, you will not make the sale.
6. Admit when you make mistakes, apologize, and move on.

"Lynette Spano Vives had to overcome the obstacles of welfare and a ghetto upbringing to become a successful businesswoman.**"**

Lynette Spano Vives
President, Chief Executive Officer,
Software Control
International, Inc.
Washington, D.C.

I always felt different and just a little special. When I was a small child growing up in the ghetto in Brooklyn, kids would pull my hair and say, "Who does she think she is?" I knew who I was and even at that young age what I didn't want—to be married with a baby by the age of twenty-one.

Growing up in the ghetto in New York was rough. My family, Cuban and Puerto Rican, tried to survive in New York City but my mother did not speak English. Because of this she could not find a job and the family was forced to take assistance from the welfare system in New York. It was a humiliating experience and after three years of being on welfare, she said, "I am too proud, I have got to get off this." I learned a lot from my mother about being goal-oriented. She showed me what it is like to be poor and to be afraid of poverty.

An Early Entrepreneur

I knew immediately that there had to be more to life than hand-me-down clothes and going to charity homes and having holes in my shoes. When I was nine I set up my first profit-making center. My twin brother and I built a shoeshine box. I went to the local park and had my brother and three boys shine shoes for me and for every quarter they made, I kept a dime. I was making a commission at age nine. That showed me that if you want something badly enough you can get it—providing you want it badly enough.

In high school I opened a small sweater franchise. After going to college for a short time I worked as a model and then as a receptionist, secretary, and stewardess for United Airlines until I was laid off. I did not know what to do with myself next. Since I didn't have an education there were a few doors that were going to be closed to me. My next door neighbor at the time suggested I work for a computer software company, Lifeboat Associates, in New York City. I started as a salesperson earning $150 a week even though I did not know anything about computers or software. I thought a computer was a television set with a wire and that diskettes were a type of record.

At Lifeboat I met Jeff Baltimore, who is vice-president of my firm today. He was hired by Lifeboat at the same time I was and he convinced me in the beginning to stick it out there as a salesperson.

One of the things I did at Lifeboat was to reorganize their call system. Calls were coming in but no one was keeping track of them. I put together a reference and call back system to service our clients faster and better. In ten months Jeff and I took over the department. In eighteen months I went from a salary of $150 a week to $60,000 year and brought in $2.5 million for the company.

In the process I began to develop a barracuda instinct, going after clients. That's when I got my nickname "Coach." I used to bring all the salespeople together in my department and challenge them, "Give me your best lead," or "Give me your toughest sale." When they did, I would get on the phone right there in front of them and make a sale. I got them competing with me. There was envy, but there was also respect.

The reason I did so well at Lifeboat was that I firmly believed that there was nothing in life I could not do, providing I wanted it badly enough. Even though I did not know what software was and I did not know what a word processor was I knew there was a need and I recognized that it does not matter if you are selling software applications, lipsticks, or consulting services: if you service the needs of your clients, they are going to come back. My clients all came back.

After I had been at Lifeboat for two years, a key person in the company asked Jeff, "How do feel that there's a woman making more than you and that she is also Hispanic?" Jeff was upset but I was angry and resigned. They asked me to stay but I was through. I went home where my mother looked at me and said "Where have I failed? Not only are you twenty-six and not married, but you're unemployed and I can't afford to take care of you."

I had saved some money while at Lifeboat and in 1983 Jeff and I founded Software Control International. I had learned a lot at Lifeboat about the industry and servicing clients, but I thought there were better ways to run a business. Most entrepreneurs have the attitude, "I think I can run this better than my boss."

When we started the company, I got a friend to deliver software products to my mother's house, even though I did not have enough money to pay for them up front. For our first client we went into the presentation with all the gusto of a much larger firm. They found it hard to believe we were only a three-person operation. After being in operation for four months, we received a contract for $10 million.

Software Control specializes in providing services to the federal government. Software had some advantages in that it qualifies for 95-507, the federal law that states that any company that sells to the United States government must subcontract a certain percentage of its products to minority-owned firms. Software Control has become a company that scouts the marketplace for software requirements, then tests and evaluates the product and recommends applications as well as provides software training.

I do not believe I will ever feel that I have really made it. Maybe it will hit me if I get on the cover of *Time*, but then I will probably want to be on the cover of *Life*.

TIPS FOR SUCCESS

1. Focus. Be goal oriented.
2. Understand the commodity that you are interested in.
3. Know your competition.
4. Find the nature of what people want, find out why those commodities are needed, and get them to the people.
5. You must be extremely confident and believe in yourself.
6. You've got to believe that no one can do better than yourself.
7. It takes a special woman who can lose $1000 in a day of business and say "so what?" Every day is a different day. It may not look good today, but it can't get any worse if you believe in yourself and your potential. I am a firm believer that nothing can stop someone who is determined.

"Frankie Welch overcame a lack of capital and provided women with the best of American sportswear and clothes.**"**

Frankie Welch
President,
Frankie Welch Textile Designs
Alexandria, Virginia

M y first and major store became a reality twenty-three years ago when I bought an eighteenth-century (1749) house in Alexandria, Virginia.

My involvement in fashion and design was a spur to owning my own business and when I found the house I knew it was the right place. I borrowed to get started and opened the doors with a lot of hope in my heart. I soon found out that there was a need for my type of shop where women could come and meet their friends without any sales pressure—an atmosphere of conviviality where you can have a cup of coffee and get honest advice about what to wear and what really looks good on you. My philosophy at the shop from the beginning was that we treat everyone warmly and give everyone attention whether they are high level leaders or housewives. Through the years we have dressed Congressional wives, their daughters, their granddaughters, members of the Cabinet, leading women executives, and foreign dignitaries.

My goal was to have the house serve as a true American dress shop with the best of American sportswear and clothes. Not at the $3,000 level, but at the medium price level, which is what this country does best.

Beginning a Business

When I opened the store on September 12, 1963—I had a following. Many people, including Congressional wives, had taken my course on how to coordinate your own wardrobe and how to look your best, without spending a lot of money. It was a very successful class and I taught it at several universities. I also had traveled to France as part of a successful fashion competition that I had won. There had been many media stories about my seminars and this translated into customers to sustain my business.

Cherokee Alphabet Scarf

My store was four years old when my Cherokee Alphabet scarf was unveiled at The Virginia Museum, and portrayed my Cherokee heritage. Mrs. Dean Rusk (wife of the Secretary of State in 1967) requested an all-American design for President and Mrs. Johnson to give to visiting heads of state. The Secretary and Mrs. Rusk also used this scarf as an official gift. For the first time an American theme, the Cherokee Alphabet printed on a textile, was used as a presidential gift.

Mrs. Johnson later invited me to the White House and asked me to design a scarf that would celebrate her "Discover America" project. I designed the scarf immediately with a "Discover America" theme. She also asked if I thought it would be appropriate to have a fashion show in the White House for the governors' wives to promote "Discover America." I said, "Mrs. Johnson, the fashion industry has been wishing for years for this invitation." The 150 scarves for the governors' wives and the press were hand painted on time and the day was a success.

A White House Tradition

Betty Ford was also a good customer of mine when she was a Congressional wife and a First Lady. In fact she helped unveil my book on Indian jewelry. When she was going to China with President Ford I suggested that she take along a cosmetic case to hold a lovely pink and green silk hostess dress. We rolled the dress up until it fit in the case. "This way," I said, "if your luggage gets lost you will at least have an extra dress and your makeup with you at all times."

When she returned she told me that her luggage did get lost somewhere in northern China. She wore the dress to a black-tie dinner—it was very elegant—and the day was saved. Part of success, I believe, is putting yourself in the customer's place, thinking through what she will be doing and the places she will be visiting.

Many of our customers travel constantly on business and we help them with their wardrobes, what to pack, how to pack the minimum and still feel well dressed for every occasion.

Today, in addition to my original shop, I also have a dress shop right across the street from the White House and the Old Executive Office Building where administration staffers and Washingtonians can shop during the day. I have designed commemorative items such as scarves and men's ties for the past six presidents and did the inaugural scarf for President Reagan's first and second terms. My most exciting and rewarding assignment was when I designed Betty Ford's dress that is now in the Smithsonian First Ladies Collection.

Important Ingredient for Entrepreneurs

When people ask me about entrepreneurship, I tell them that the strongest thing that I had when I started, which would be the strongest thing I have now, is my expertise and ability to fill a need in the marketplace. Of course, you can never have a guarantee that there will be a market for your product or services. You reach a point where you must take the plunge and do it. If you are just in it for the money, you will be very disappointed, so you had better love what you are doing.

This is a very important ingredient for any entrepreneur—love of your work. This is what I try to convey when I teach. Today my teaching is divided among seven universities, including Winthrop College where they have a Frankie Welch design room that houses 3,000 pieces.

My daughter Genie is buying my businesses from me and will be running the retail store and doing all the buying. I am very proud that Genie is carrying on the entrepreneurial tradition. When she was a child we would discuss every aspect of the business around the dinner table. We all listened to one another and learned about our day's events. This was one way that I could share the business with my family so that they would feel part of the success.

New Challenges

To meet the needs of my design clients (many of whom are presidents of corporations, museums, universities and hospitals) I have developed another business which is a center for information for real property and businesses for sale. My challenge now is teaching in addition to consulting for corporations. I work with the president or vice-president of the corporation and develop taste level studies. I help management to define the corporate image as it appears to the customer, client, or consumer. What can they do to improve their corporation? I analyze everything from traffic flow within the corporation to the effectiveness of the support staff in dealing with the public.

Success begins with you. This means you must invest in yourself, your clothes, your voice—how do you appear to others? Are you a happy or negative person? Also, as an entrepreneur try to delegate whenever you can. This will free you to do those things that only you can do. I also believe very strongly that you must be kind to those around you—kindness and manners play a very strong part in any success.

If you are starting out try to work for the person you admire the most in the career you want to have. Work as hard as you can and learn, learn, learn. If it's in the design field work in the workroom at any level—even if you are just assigned to pick up lint and pencils. Read the trade publications and all the newspapers.

The one thing I had to overcome was lack of capital in the beginning. I had to work hard to keep my capital invested in myself, putting all of the money and profit back into the business. I succeeded because of quality and innovation. Just remember the old rule: If you have a different, high-quality product, people will beat a path to your door.

TIPS FOR SUCCESS

1. Have a detail person, someone who will take care of all the petty details. This will free you to do the important things.
2. Invest in yourself—invest in your clothes, your voice, and your whole image.
3. Be happy with yourself and share a positive attitude with others.
4. Have a social conscience—do good whenever you can.
5. Be kind to those around you and treat everyone with respect.
6. In your first job, get experience. Work, at whatever level, with the person whom you admire most. Learn everything you can from that person.
7. When you finally get into business, and are running your own company, be sure to hire the best people possible for the job, regardless of what you have to pay them.
8. Have a bookkeeper and an accountant, but know how to read the books.
9. Have some quiet time every day so that you can get geared up for the tasks ahead.

"The two biggest obstacles Louise Woerner overcame were fear of failure *and* fear of success.**"**

Louise Woerner
Owner, President, HCR, Inc.
Rochester, New York

An entrepreneur since 1978, I am president and owner of HCR, a company that provides home care services in Rochester, New York, with a Washington office performing research and management consulting. Through daily exposure to the issues confronting the health care industry, we at HCR have developed a management technique for improving the productivity of home care workers. At the federal level, we have expanded our analytical base well beyond health issues into energy and defense. This success in business has afforded me the opportunity to serve on the Private Industry Council in Monroe County, New York, on advisory boards to the New York Federal Reserve and Chase Lincoln First Bank, and as a member of several women's organizations such as Zonta International. The award my staff presented to me in 1983 for being their fearless leader is something of which I am especially proud because it reflects their understanding of the risks and challenges I have faced as a woman entrepreneur.

Familiar Obstacles

The obstacles I have overcome throughout my career are familiar to many women. I was one of the first women to receive a master's degree in business administration from the University of Chicago, and the only woman in my graduating class.

Throughout my education, I was fortunate to receive the sound advice of several people. I still seek advice from Ray S. Erlandson, who was chairman of the Department of Business Administration at Trinity University when I did my undergraduate work there. He shared stories of the business world with me, and impressed upon me the importance of the American values of hard work and honesty in a competitive environment. He also taught me the importance of the old boys network, and emphasized that business opportunities could arise from unexpected places. For example, he had met a business associate at church, and they would exchange information between hymns.

I also owe a great deal to the dean of students at the University of Chicago, where I received my master's degree. He cut the Gordian knot for me by increasing my scholarship which enabled me to finish the work necessary for my master's.

After three years of consulting experience in Dallas, I applied for a job at a major consulting firm in New York City that had hired some of my classmates right out of school. Although the firm said I did exceptionally well on the interviews and tests, it decided it just wasn't ready to hire a woman. Years later, when forming my own company, I was denied a $10,000 loan from a bank in my home town despite more than adequate collateral. I began the business anyway by charging office furniture and supplies on my MasterCard.

Tenacity and Ability

Women in business soon learn that the free enterprise system offers a great deal of opportunity if they have the tenacity and ability to compete effectively. The demands imposed on an entrepreneur, however, are not for everyone. At many points in the development of the firm, I have had all-or-nothing choices. The question was not the simple one of deciding to stabilize or grow. The interesting question has always been whether to continue to play the game or try to take my cash out. These choices have been difficult ones since each moderate step in the business cycle required a quantum leap in mental preparation for the new challenges: accepting increased financial risk, committing more time, and finding exceptional people.

Stories of successful entrepreneurs and managers give me the inspiration and courage to proceed. In reading Ray Kroc's *Grinding It Out*, I could relate to Kroc's inability to succeed with his favorite sandwich, the Hawaiian burger—pineapple on a bun with no burger. I could not help but think that, just like the Hawaiian burger, some of my best ideas were ahead of their time. Several authors have made the point that when the barriers excluding women from the opportunities of free enterprise are removed, that does not mean they will be let in or be able to stay in the game. In *The Managerial Woman*, Margaret Hennig and Anne Jardin gave the invaluable advice that in order to compete successfully, women must not only be as competent as men, but must firmly believe that they are.

Two Kinds of Fear

My experience has generally confirmed this advice—that losing some battles is part of the war, and that fear must be managed. As the management textbooks suggest, I have planned my work and worked my plan, but not without difficulty. Though the planning and the problems are familiar to both men and women, frequently the experiences of women entrepreneurs are very different from those of their male counterparts: women experience more fear and insecurity. I am reminded of that old joke: Ask a man where he bought a steak and he will say "Joe's Grocery." Ask a woman the same question, and she will say, "Why? What's wrong with it?" I am still trying to understand how that fear, of both failure and success, has been an important motivator for me. But I also realize that fear creates excitement, like that feeling when you are looking down a five-story drop from the top of a roller coaster. The uncertainty is part of the fun and my most familiar emotion.

HCR is now doing well after seven years, as are many businesses owned by women. In general, however, small businesses involve enormous risks. Most of them fail within five years, and women business owners still have far to go. When I read the *State of Small Business 1985*, the statistic that struck me the most was that less than 1 percent of women entrepreneurs gross more than $100,000 annually. Therefore, progress must be made through continuation of our individual and collective efforts to participate in the business sector of the economy.

The risks and the rewards are real. I would encourage women to take the risk of entering business and experience the reward of taking on the challenges they construct for themselves. The victories won by the hard-working women who have preceded us have made many new opportunities available. Now in the future, the vision must be our own.

TIPS FOR SUCCESS

1. Always remember that business is very demanding for men and women. It's not that you think it is difficult—it is difficult.
2. You will not win every battle. The losses are not personal failures or even business failures—they are part of the game.
3. Be aware that your style is always observed critically. Few people have the full range of business tools at their disposal, so be careful how you use anger and aggressiveness in negotiations.
4. Don't expect everyone to be necessarily pleased at your success. Develop ways to celebrate your successes and take time to note when you've done well.
5. Keep yourself open to ideas and opportunities.
6. Work hard and do a good job.

NWEA

The National Women's Economic Alliance serves as a resource to women in business. We would like to hear from you about your experiences in business, whether as a business owner or career woman within industry. For information about the alliance send a stamped, self-addressed envelope to:

> National Women's Economic Alliance
> 605 14th Street, N.W.
> Washington, D.C. 20005